TRUMP UNVEILED

TRUMP
UNVEILED

EXPOSING THE
BIGOTED BILLIONAIRE

JOHN K. WILSON

OR Books
New York · London

© 2016 John K. Wilson

Published for the book trade by OR Books in partnership with
Counterpoint Press.
Distributed to the trade by Publishers Group West

All rights information: rights@orbooks.com

All references and sources posted online at trumpunveiled.com and
johnkwilson.com.

First printing 2016

Cataloging-in-Publication data is available from the Library of Congress.
A catalog record for this book is available from the British Library.

ISBN 978-1-944869-31-1

Text design by Under|Over. Typeset by AarkMany Media, Chennai, India.

10 9 8 7 6 5 4 3 2 1

To my parents

TABLE OF CONTENTS

INTRODUCTION:
TRUMP THE NARCISSIST ···· 11

CHAPTER 1:
LYING TRUMP ············ 23

CHAPTER 2:
BANKRUPT TRUMP ········ 51

CHAPTER 3:
TYRANT TRUMP ·········· 93

CHAPTER 4:
PARANOID TRUMP ······· 111

CHAPTER 5:
RACIST TRUMP ·········· 141

CHAPTER 6:
SEXIST TRUMP ·········· 171

CHAPTER 7:
CARELESS TRUMP ······· 211

CONCLUSION:
THE TRUMP GAMBLE ···· 231

public figures of the past several decades. He has been routinely insulted, ridiculed, and treated as a punchline, and yet Trump and his wife still hold this delusional belief that he is almost universally beloved.

Trump's narcissism also explains why he is a flip-flopper on so many issues. For a narcissist like Trump, the only thing that matters is what helps Trump. Being ideologically consistent doesn't matter. Because Trump is a narcissist, he is willing to say and do anything to increase his chances of gaining power. And so Trump will take any position (and change any previous position) that will help him "in the moment." Trump's narcissism also means that he thinks he is incapable of being wrong. Therefore, when he changes a position in order to gain an advantage, Trump conveniently forgets whatever his past position was.

TRUMP THE BULLY

Trump once said, "When I look at myself in the first grade and I look at myself now, I'm basically the same." Most people don't peak emotionally at age six, but Trump has been a bully his entire life and perhaps this is what he is referencing. A report about his childhood noted that "Trump could erupt in anger, pummeling another boy or smashing a baseball bat if he made an out." One child who lived next door was warned by his mother to "stay away from the Trumps." He later explained that "Donald was known to be a bully, I was a little kid, and my parents didn't want me beaten up." One day, his mother found Donald throwing rocks at him in his playpen.

Trump once wrote that as a second-grader, he "actually" gave his music teacher a black eye because "I didn't think he knew anything about music, and I almost got expelled." The music teacher, Charles Walker, said that Trump never hit him, but did say about Trump that "When that kid was ten, even then he was a little shit."

Ironically, Trump claimed that anecdotes in Ben Carson's book showed "he's got a pathological temper or temperament" and added that violent tendencies should disqualify a presidential candidate: "I don't want somebody that hit somebody in the face really hard…"

Trump's abusive behavior caused him to be sent to New York Military Academy where "they'd smack the hell out of you," and he laughed at his classmates when they spoke to put them in their place. His experience only made him more arrogant: "When I graduated, I was a very elite person."

Trump offers advice for how to deal with bullies: "I learned it in high school, you've got to hit a bully really hard, really strongly, right between the eyes." However, that's also good advice for how to be a bully.

What makes Trump a bully is not just how he treats his enemies, but also how he treats everyone else. Trump recalls how he dealt with one of his friends who had an apartment in his building. He learned that there was a termination clause in the lease and "just for fun" decided to invoke it and extort a higher rent from him along with a $50,000 donation to a charity Trump liked.

Trump's acts of petty revenge are legendary, and he is proud of them. He recalled how one of his golf courses let an aspiring PGA player practice there. When the player made it to the PGA tour, Trump wanted him to wear the Trump logo for free. Merely because the golfer said that he would need to check with his agent, Trump banned him from his golf courses, and then proudly bragged about the incident.

Trump wrote "My motto is: Always get even. When somebody screws you, screw them back in spades." According to him, "Getting even is not always a personal thing. It's just a part of doing business."

As the rich owner of a private business, Trump never faced anyone who could stand up against him. Any employee who disagreed with him would get fired for "disloyalty." His ex-employees and ex-wives have been kept quiet with non-disclosure agreements and the threat of lawsuits. Even his children can't criticize Trump without risking their lucrative positions and billion-dollar inheritance.

Trump declared, "When you are in business you need to get even with people who screw you. You need to screw them back fifteen times harder." This is the bully's creed: viciously attack anyone who stands up against you, to teach a lesson to everyone else.

THE NARCISSIST-IN-CHIEF

Trump's narcissism is part of what makes him so dumb. Because Trump thinks he's a genius who knows everything and is always right, he's incapable of learning. His views on public policy generally range from the ignorant to the idiotic.

Trump's refusal to admit that he's ever wrong is another dangerous personality trait that's part of his narcissism. The *Washington Post* fact-checker declared that "There's never been a presidential candidate like Donald Trump—someone so cavalier about the facts and so unwilling to ever admit error, even in the face of overwhelming evidence."

Trump's propensity for surrounding himself with yes men is another problematic character flaw. By demanding absolute agreement with his ideas, Trump creates a culture of groupthink that makes it almost impossible to challenge his misguided views. Bill Pruitt, a producer on Seasons 1 and 2 of *The Apprentice*, said: "He was always a narcissist, you can see that." According to his ghostwriter Tony Schwartz, Trump's need for attention is "completely compulsive." A Trump casino executive noted his "volatile and unpredictable moods." At his Atlantic City marina, Trump kicked a wooden platform into the water because he didn't like the paint color and yelled, "This place is a shithouse."

Perhaps Trump's worst trait is his belief that he knows everything and is the best at everything. Even for a genius and a superstar athlete, such arrogance is a dangerous flaw. For an idiot like Trump, believing he knows everything is catastrophic. Instead of listening to experts, carefully weighing evidence, and waiting until facts are known, Trump will always tend to immediately trust his worst instincts.

Trump regularly brags about attending the University of Pennsylvania: "I went to an Ivy League school. I'm very highly educated. I know words, I have the best words." At the same time, Trump dismisses expertise and education: "I love the poorly educated. We're the smartest people, we're the most loyal people."

Trump is fond of praising his own intelligence: "Sorry losers and haters, but my IQ is one of the highest—and you all know it! Please don't feel so stupid or insecure, it's not your fault." Trump claimed that he inherited a brilliant mind because of genetics: "I had an uncle, went to MIT, who is a top professor. Dr. John Trump. A genius. It's in my blood. I'm smart. Great marks. Like really smart." According to Trump: "Good genes, very good genes. Okay, very smart."

Part of Trump's narcissism is his belief that he knows more about every topic than anyone else: "I know more about #ISIS than the generals do, believe me." Trump even claimed to be the world's leading expert on energy issues: "I know more about renewables than any human being on earth because I understand it from a practical viewpoint."

Trump is such a narcissist that even monumental political events are only viewed by Trump in terms of how they affect him personally. After Britain voted to leave the European Union, sending stocks worldwide crashing down, Trump sent out a fundraising appeal: "We're going to do the exact same thing on Election Day 2016 here in the United States of America....Let's send another shockwave around the world." Trump saw the devastating economic effects on Great Britain as a profitable opportunity for his golf course in Scotland: "If the pound goes down, more people are coming to Turnberry, frankly. For traveling and for other things, I think it very well could turn out to be positive." When a reporter noted that "the country is not a golf course," Trump replied: "No, it's not, but you'd be amazed how similar it is." In Trump's self-centered view, what's good for his golf course is good for a country.

THE MYSTERY OF THE FAKE TRUMP

"It was not me on the phone."

That was how Donald Trump responded to the 1991 audio recording of him pretending to be his own press agent, using the generic-sounding fake name of "John Miller."

Trump called the report a "scam." He declared, "No, I don't know anything about it." Initially, Trump offered only a vague denial: "It doesn't sound like my voice at all. I have many, many people that are trying to imitate my voice. And you can imagine that. And this sounds like one of these scams, one of the many scams. It doesn't sound like me." Trump added, "I don't think it was me. It doesn't sound like me. I don't know even what they're talking about. I have no idea."

When Trump was asked again if he would plant stories with reporters using the alias John Miller or John Barron, Trump replied more emphatically, "No, and it was not me on the phone. It was not me on the phone. And it doesn't sound like me on the phone, I will tell you that. And it was not me on the phone."

Trump responded to questions by insulting anyone in the media who dared ask him about it: "You mean you are going so low as to talk about something that took place 25 years ago, about whether or not I made a phone call? I guess you're saying under a presumed name." Trump was definitive: "The answer is no."

It sure seemed like Trump on the phone, and if that is the case, he is knowingly lying about his past use of aliases. No one could expect Trump to remember if he made a phone call 25 years ago. But no one could imagine that Trump would forget pretending to be his own publicist in order to plant stories in the media about his sexual prowess.

There are many arguments to suggest that Trump today is lying. First, in the call "John Miller" sounds very much like Donald Trump, complete with Trump's unique self-aggrandizing obsession ("He's starting to do tremendously well financially. As you saw, he got his licenses five to nothing the other day and totally unanimous.") Second, "John Miller" knew all kinds of intimate details about Donald Trump. Third, numerous journalists from the 1970s through the 1990s recount receiving calls from "John Miller" or "John Barron" and relate that these calls sounded tremendously like Trump himself. In 1990, Trump testified in a court case that "I believe on occasion I used that name."

Finally, Trump has already admitted that he was "John Miller." *People* magazine at the time reported that it was "Donald Trump, posing as a fictitious PR man." They played the tape of Donald pretending to John Miller for Marla Maples, and she immediately recognized his voice and didn't like what he said about her. Later, Trump apologized to *People*, admitting what he had done. Here's how *People* described it: "The John Miller fiasco he called a joke gone awry. 'What I did became a good time at Marla's expense, and I'm very sorry,' says the newly humbled tycoon. As for his wandering eye, 'I'd felt that I needed space and freedom after the divorce, so I took the opportunity to go out with other women, but I kept coming back to Marla. I realized, why go looking for something when you already have exactly what you want?'"

We know the voice is Trump's because he confessed it to Sue Carswell of *People* magazine: "He said he was sorry he'd done it. He asked if I would go out as a sort of apology with him and Marla. We went to one of the hot clubs at the time." He picked her up in his stretch limo. According to Carswell, "There's no doubt in my mind that he apologized to me and that he made it clear that he was the man on the tape." *People* magazine printed this apology, and Trump never objected.

In response to a question about Marla Maples' ring, "John Miller" gave this answer: "It was never an engagement ring. It was a ring—I mean, he wouldn't buy the engagement ring. Actually, he bought the ring at the Taj Mahal at Tiffany's. The only place that

Tiffany's has that, you know, in a hotel is because of his relationship with Tiffany being the neighbor next door to Trump Tower and Tiffany decided to open up a store at the Taj Mahal. And this was a way of giving Tiffany some business in addition to getting Ivan—getting Marla something that would be nice." Only Trump could turn a question about a ring into an advertisement for his Taj Mahal.

By pretending to be "Miller," Trump was not merely lying about his identity; he was doing so in order to link himself in the press as having sex with famous women.

"Miller" said: "Ivana wants to get back with Donald....She wants to get back, she's told it to a lot of her friends and she's told it to him, but it's so highly unlikely." He added: "He's living with Marla and he's got three other girlfriends."

"Miller" said: "He's somebody that has a lot of options, and, frankly, he gets called by everybody. He gets called by everybody in the book, in terms of women," adding that "He's got a whole open field really. A lot of the people that you write about, and you people do a great job, by the way, but a lot of the people that you write about really are—I mean, they call. They just call. Actresses, people that you write about just call to see if they can go out with him and things."

Asked specifically about Madonna, "Miller" replied: "Well, she called and wanted to go out with him, that I can tell you. And one of the other people that you're writing about." "Miller" also claimed that actress Kim Basinger wanted to date Trump.

"Miller" also declared that "Now he has somebody else named Carla who is beautiful." Then "Miller" explained, "she's a very successful model" and gave her full name, Carla Bruni, saying that her "father is one of the wealthiest men in Europe" adding, "she was having a very big thing with Mick Jagger. And then what happened, she was going with Eric Clapton, and Eric Clapton introduced her to Mick Jagger, and then Mick Jagger started calling her, and she ended up going with Mick Jagger. And then she dropped Mick Jagger for Donald, and that's where it is right now."

"And again, he's not making any commitments to Carla either just so you understand," he said. "Well, they just get along very good and she's very pretty and all of that stuff. But, you know, he doesn't have any idea who she is, right? When he meets the right woman, it's going to be a great relationship and it's going to be a very, you know, because he believes strongly in the marriage concept."

Bruni did not react well to the sex rumors Trump was spreading about her, telling the press: "Trump is obviously a lunatic."

Sometimes, Trump posed as "John Barron." Trump has admitted this, saying, "You know, over the years I've used aliases. I actually used the name 'Barron' for some real estate deals." Trump also used the code name "the Baron" when he was cheating on his first wife and secretly sleeping with Marla Maples at his casinos in Atlantic City. Bizarrely enough, Trump and Melania named their son "Barron."

When asked who he was and where he came from, "Miller" offered a highly unconvincing answer: "I basically worked for different firms. I worked for a couple of different firms, and I'm somebody that he knows and I think somebody that he trusts and likes. So I'm going to do this a little part time, and then, yeah, go on with my life, too."

Trump was such a narcissist that he posed as his own PR consultant in order to promote his sexual prowess and lie about all of the famous women that were sleeping with him. Trump didn't care that he was lying, or that his fake persona made him look like a lunatic. Trump was so obsessed with talking about himself that he needed to adopt fake identities.

1 LYING TRUMP

All politicians are liars. Yet no presidential candidate has ever lied so often and with such indifference to the truth as Donald Trump. Trump has been caught in a thousand lies, but he tries to deflect his distortions and errors by simply refusing to acknowledge them. At the same time, Trump has argued that the alleged lying of his opponents is a primary reason to vote for him.

Trump called Hillary Clinton a "world-class liar" and made his supporters call Ted Cruz "Lyin' Ted," but the truth is that Trump is the biggest liar in American political history. No other figure comes close to Trump, according to the measurements of various fact-checkers.

No one lies more often, and about more petty topics, than Donald Trump. Trump often lies as if the truth is a game to him, and he wins extra points if he can find someone gullible enough to believe what he's saying. Yet at other times, Trump's determination to lie, even when no one believes him, even when the facts prove the exact opposite of what he's saying, reflects an extraordinary will to deceive. Trump is such a narcissist that in his head, the truth becomes whatever he thinks it should be.

One of Trump's lawyers told *Vanity Fair* in 1990: "Donald is a believer in the big-lie theory. If you say something again and again, people will believe you." He cannot conceive of the possibility that he could be wrong, so he reinterprets reality and history to meet whatever he thinks and says, even if that means lying about the past and present. When he can't deny reality and must acknowledge that he held a contrary view in the past, Trump simply asserts that he was in a different "role."

Trump wrote in his most recent book that "sometimes" he must make "outrageous comments and give them what they want—viewers and readers—in order to make a point." Because, he says, "I'm a businessman with a brand to sell." In Trump's world, he's always play-acting. Nobody expects a salesman to tell the complete truth.

Trump believes that lying is perfectly innocent if you're doing it to promote yourself. And his fans want to imagine he's telling the truth because he fulfills their anti-political fantasy. It may seem strange to imagine Trump as anyone's fantasy, but Trump does fulfill certain fantasies about a political candidate who is too rich to be bought, too honest to be cowed, and too radical for the establishment.

New York Post reporter Susan Mulcahy, who covered Trump during the 1990s, noted that: "Trump turned out to be the king of ersatz. Not just fake, but false. He lied about everything, with gusto." Mulcahy said, "He wanted attention, but he could not control his pathological lying....Every statement he uttered required more than the usual amount of fact-checking." In 2004, *Vanity Fair* quoted Mulcahy's view of how the media covered Trump: "I actually would sit back and be amazed at how often people would write about him in a completely gullible way. He was a great character, but he was full of crap 90 percent of the time." Remarkably, a quote from Donald Trump immediately followed: "I agree with her 100 percent."

Why is Trump such a prolific liar? One reason is that he became famous by lying. Trump got headlines by making up stories to appear in the press. Because the tabloids wanted interesting stories more than truthful ones, Trump never suffered any consequences for his lying. Trump famously called his approach "truthful hyperbole," but the emphasis was always on the hyperbole: "I play to people's fantasies. People may not always think big themselves, but they can still get very excited by those who do. That's why a little hyperbole never hurts. People want to believe that something is the biggest and the greatest and the most spectacular. I call it truthful hyperbole. It's an innocent form of exaggeration—and a very effective form of promotion."

For many of his supporters, telling them that Trump is a liar is like reminding them that reality TV shows and professional wrestling are often scripted. Why should they care? The entertainment value is enhanced by the lie, and that's what they want.

LAZY TRUMP

One reason why Trump lies so much is that he's incredibly lazy. He never bothers to research what he's said in the past, and so he frequently contradicts previous statements because he doesn't truly believe in anything.

Jeb Bush will forever be remembered as "low energy" because of Trump's constant insults, but the reality is that Trump is the low-energy candidate. That may seem like an odd description for a man who is constantly promoting himself and claims to sleep only a few hours every night. But Trump is low-energy in the sense of being intellectually indolent.

One of Trump's favorite stories is about how he was going to deliver a speech at an arena for a motivational conference, and five minutes before he arrived, he asked his driver, "What am I supposed to talk about tonight?" For him, this is an example of his brilliance: he can ad lib a speech on any topic on a moment's notice. In reality, his refusal to prepare speeches reflects his unwillingness to work.

Trump is so lazy that he doesn't even prepare sentences in his own head before he utters them. His babbling, rambling, incoherent mode of talking is a reflection of the fact that he's never had to think about what he says.

Trump is high energy when it comes to talking about Donald Trump. But he is extraordinarily low energy at researching anything, preparing his ideas, or thinking deeply about anything.

Trump has declared, "Life is not all sincerity. Life is an act, to a large extent."

Trump is someone who spent eight months running as a candidate in the Republican primary without bothering to think about his position about abortion beyond his rehearsed soundbite. When pressed by Chris Matthews, Trump wrongly guessed that the anti-abortion movement he had belatedly joined for political reasons wanted to declare that women should be arrested for having abortions.

MOCKING THE DISABLED

When Donald Trump mocked a *New York Times* reporter for his physical disability, imitating his impaired arm movements, it was a shocking example of how petty and vile he could be. But the most fascinating aspect of the entire sleazy episode was how Trump was willing to lie over and over again in an attempt to pretend that he had never done this.

Trump claimed he had seen television reports about "thousands" of Arabs in New Jersey celebrating the 9/11 attacks. When everybody pointed out that Trump was wrong, he desperately searched for any evidence that this happened, and stumbled upon a *Washington Post* report by Serge Kovaleski that mentioned police in New Jersey "questioned a number of people who were allegedly seen celebrating the attacks." But when Kovaleski observed that none of the reports were confirmed, and that they never approached the "thousands" of people celebrating on TV that Trump claimed to see, Trump turned upon him.

At a rally, Trump mocked Kovaleski, who suffers from arthrogryposis, which limits the movement of his arms, and causes his hands to be in a very distinctive position. Trump did an imitation of Kovaleski's physical disability while mocking what he said. In response, Trump was widely criticized.

But instead of apologizing, Trump tried to deny that he had done what he did. Trump declared in a statement, "I have no idea who this reporter, Serge Kovalski (sic) is, what he looks like or his level of intelligence. I merely mimicked what I thought would be a flustered reporter trying to get out of a statement he made long ago."

In reality, Kovaleski had interviewed Trump dozens of times as a *New York Daily News* reporter in the late 1980s and had been on a first-name basis with him. Trump asserted, "Despite having one of the all-time great memories I certainly do not remember him." Trump claimed, "Serge Kovaleski must think a lot of himself if he thinks I remember him from decades ago—if I ever met him at all, which I doubt I did." It's heartening to imagine that Trump is so committed to equality that he doesn't see obvious physical disabilities; but nobody really believes this. At another rally, Trump said of Kovaleski, "he changed the article, he said he made a mistake." Kovaleski never changed the article and never said he made a mistake. But Trump asserted, "I didn't know what he looked like. I didn't know he was disabled. I didn't know it.

I didn't know it at all." Trump claimed to be doing an imitation of a reporter "groveling."

With his bent hand, he was clearly doing a very specific imitation of Kovaleski. This fact is confirmed by what Trump said during the imitation: "the poor guy, you gotta see this guy."

If Trump had no idea what Kovaleski looked like and had never seen him before, why would he say, "you gotta see this guy"? Clearly, Trump was claiming to be doing a physical re-enactment of how Kovaleski reacted, which would be impossible unless Trump had seen him. If Trump didn't remember who Kovaleski was, why did he suddenly imitate someone with a disability? It was perfectly clear that Kovaleski had a disability, even if Trump somehow didn't remember meeting this man with a disability dozens of times. Trump's gesticulations only made sense if he were trying to mock Kovaleski's disability.

And why would Trump call him "the poor guy"? The only reason why Trump would call Kovaleski a "poor guy" is because Trump knew he had a physical disability and was trying to convey some sympathy for him (while denouncing him and ridiculing his physical appearance).

Although mocking the physical afflictions of the disabled is certainly rude, the worst part of this story is that it shows how far Trump is willing to go in defense of a lie. Merely to avoid some criticism, Trump pretended not to know a reporter, and fabricated a completely unbelievable story to deny the truth. If Trump was willing to create such an intricate series of lies to cover up a minor embarrassment to himself, what might he do to cover up actual wrongdoing if he were president? If you can't believe what Trump says about Kovaleski, what can you believe that he says?

TRUMP'S INVASIONS

Donald Trump has convinced many people that he had opposed foreign interventions and will keep America out of war, citing Iraq and Libya as examples where Hillary Clinton supported a military intervention that he opposed. In reality, Trump was one of the biggest cheerleaders for war in Iraq and Libya, and now he's lying to conceal what he said in the past.

In 2016, Trump blamed Hillary Clinton because she "get rid of Gaddafi, for what reason?" Trump praised Gaddafi and Saddam Hussein because "they killed terrorists." Trump claimed about Clinton, "She's killed hundreds of thousands of people with her stupidity."

But in 2011, Trump complained on his video blog that Obama and Clinton were too slow to intervene in Libya: "I can't believe what our country is doing. Gaddafi in Libya is killing thousands of people, nobody knows how bad it is, and we're sitting around, we have soldiers all have the Middle East, and we're not bringing them in to stop this horrible carnage and that's what it is: It's a carnage.... You talk about things that have happened in history; this could be one of the worst.

Now we should go in, we should stop this guy, which would be very easy and very quick. We could do it surgically, stop him from doing it, and save these lives. This is absolutely nuts. We don't want to get involved and you're gonna end up with something like you've never seen before." Trump explained, "We should do on a humanitarian basis, immediately go into Libya, knock this guy out very quickly, very surgically, very effectively, and save the lives."

In 2016, Trump denied ever supporting the overthrow of Gaddafi: "I never discussed that subject. I was in favor of Libya? We would be so much better off if Gaddafi were in charge right now. If these politicians went to the beach and didn't do a thing and we had Saddam Hussein and we had Gaddafi in charge, instead of having terrorism all over the place, we'd be—at least they killed terrorists, all right?" Actually, Gaddafi didn't kill terrorists. To the contrary, he admitted Libya's responsibility for the 1988 Lockerbie bombing of Pan Am 103, which killed 270 people, including 189 Americans.

For Trump, the fact that he previously demanded a military invasion of Libya is tossed down the memory hole. He seemingly has no idea that he supported the overthrow of Gaddafi, now that he thinks Gaddafi would be the perfect leader for Libya.

Although Trump now says that he would have propped up Gaddafi as a dictator, Trump previously claimed that Obama should have cut a deal with the Libyan rebels, demanding 50% of Libya's oil for 25 years in exchange for American military support, and complained that, "Our leaders are too brainless to negotiate a deal like that." Trump treats stealing a nation's oil by signing a contract with a rebel military group as if it were the easiest thing in the world: "if we had been smart and negotiated shrewdly, we would have taken 50 percent of Libya's oil for twenty-five years before we spent mountains of American money."

Trump continues to lie about Libya. In his prepared foreign policy speech on April 27, 2016, Trump declared: "now ISIS is making millions of dollars a week selling Libyan oil." David Mack, an expert on Libya and terrorism with the nonpartisan Middle East Institute, called Trump's claim "absolutely untrue." And then Trump announced, "I'll take the oil," which certainly raises the question, if Trump plans to simply steal Middle East oil, why does he want to sign contracts where America only steals half of this oil?

Trump's contradictory foreign policy also applies to Egypt. In his 2016 foreign policy speech, Trump denounced Obama for supporting the downfall of corrupt Egyptian president Hosni Mubarak: "He supported the ouster of a friendly regime in Egypt that had a longstanding peace treaty with Israel, and then helped bring the Muslim Brotherhood to power in its place." But in 2011, Trump also supported Mubarak's ouster: "it's a good thing that they got him out."

TRUMP'S WAR ON IRAQ

The myth that Trump opposed the war in Iraq is one of the most frequent lies Trump tells. Trump said about Hillary Clinton, "She's the one who raised her hand for the war in Iraq and I'm the one who has been fighting it from the beginning." There were some people fighting against the war in Iraq from the beginning, but Trump definitely wasn't one of them. To the contrary, Trump had been supporting war in Iraq for more than a decade, and only began criticizing it when things went badly.

Trump declared that the invasion of Iraq was "one of the worst decisions in the history of our country, perhaps the worst." But contrary to what he claims now, it was a decision he embraced. On Sept. 11, 2002, Trump was asked if he supported invading Iraq, and his answer was, "Yeah, I guess so" and added a reference to his past support for an invasion of Iraq: "I wish the first time it was done correctly." On the first day of the war, Trump praised it as a "tremendous success from a military standpoint" and predicted the stock market would "go up like a rocket."

By March 25, 2003, Trump was declaring, "The war's a mess" after the US mistakenly shot down a British jet. But that was a critique of the way the war was fought. Even by Sept. 11, 2003, Trump did not explicitly oppose the war in Iraq, saying, "It wasn't a mistake to fight terrorism and fight it hard, and I guess maybe if I had to do it, I would have fought terrorism but not necessarily Iraq." On Nov. 4, 2003, Trump supported Bush and the war in

Iraq: "he is on a course that has to stay." On Dec. 15, 2003, Trump said about the war, "Some people agree and some people don't agree, but we are there. And if we are there, you have to take down Saddam Hussein." And even if Trump was now slightly skeptical about starting the war, he was firmly opposed to ending it: "we are there now, we have to stay, we have to win, otherwise we just won't have the same respect."

By April 16, 2004, Trump had re-written history to proclaim himself an opponent of the war: "I was never a fan of Iraq, going in, because, this guy used to keep the terrorists out. He'd kill the terrorists." And Trump espoused a theory that certain countries must be run by dictators: "to think that when we leave, it's gonna be this nice democratic country. I mean, gimme a break. There's usually a reason why a country is run a certain way." This is a particularly dangerous mindset in a president, to imagine that totalitarian rule is essential for some countries.

In 2016, when Trump was pressed to explain his comments, he said: "what I mean by that is it almost shouldn't have been done and, you know, I really don't even know what I mean, because that was a long time ago and who knows what was in my head?"

In a 2016 CNN Town Hall, Trump tried, and failed, to explain what he was thinking: "When you're in the private sector, you know, you get asked things and, you know, you're not a politician and probably the first time I was asked. By the time the war started, I was against it. And shortly thereafter, I was really against it."

During a 2016 Republican debate, Trump declared: "I'm the only one on this stage that said, 'Do not go into Iraq. Do not attack Iraq.' Nobody else on this stage said that. And I said it loud and strong. And I was in the private sector. I wasn't a politician, fortunately. But I said it, and I said it loud and clear, 'You'll destabilize the Middle East.' That's exactly what happened."

That's exactly what didn't happen. Trump never said it "loud and strong." In fact, no one ever stepped forward to say that they ever heard Trump say anything like that, even privately. He certainly never opposed the war in Iraq publicly. And while hundreds of millions of people around the world actually opposed the war in Iraq, Trump lies when he says: "I'm one of the few who was right on Iraq."

By contrast, Hillary Clinton warned that an invasion of Iraq was "fraught with danger" and noted that "after shots are fired and bombs are dropped, not all consequences are predictable." Clinton's mistake was to trust George W. Bush; Trump, by contrast, was far more militaristic than Bush, and had consistently called for an invasion of Iraq for more than a decade.

Many times in the 1990s, Trump criticized George H.W. Bush for failing to extend the Persian Gulf War and overthrow Saddam Hussein, even though doing so would have required a massive intervention, enormous numbers of dead Iraqis, and resulted in precisely the same chaotic situation that led Trump to conclude that we would be better off with Saddam left in control today. In 1999, Trump declared, "I wish he'd finished the war." Even before 9/11, and without the excuse of finding any weapons of mass destruction, Trump endorsed invading Iraq. In his 2000 book, Trump expressed his support for attacking Iraq to "carry the mission to its conclusion." Trump explicitly endorsed invading Iraq and overthrowing Saddam Hussein because "after each pounding from U.S. warplanes, Iraq has dusted itself off and gone right back to work developing a nuclear arsenal....if we decide a strike against Iraq is necessary, it is madness not to carry the mission to its conclusion."

This makes Trump far more of a military interventionist than even George W. Bush, who didn't invade Iraq until after the 9/11 attack. Trump also wrote about how George H.W. Bush was right to attack Iraq: "I only wish, however, that he had spent three more days and properly finished the job. It is this kind of will and determination to use our strength strategically that America needs again in dealing with the North Koreans." That certainly sounds like Trump would also support a military invasion of nuclear-armed North Korea to overthrow its government.

Iraq, Syria, and North Korea are not the only places where Trump endorses massive military action. In 2011, Trump wrote, "Iran's nuclear program must be stopped—by any and all means necessary. Period....Better now than later!" He added, "the only way to eliminate the Iranian nuclear threat is to bomb their facilities." If Iran must be stopped and the only way to stop is with a massive bombing campaign (since Trump firmly opposed the Obama Administration's deal with Iran), then we must add Iran to the remarkably long list of places where Trump promises to start wars.

Sometimes, it's not even clear which country Trump is planning to bomb. During one debate, Trump announced: "Iran is taking over Iraq 100 percent, so I say this: We bomb the hell out of them, take the oil. We thereby take their wealth, they have so much money—they have so much better Internet connections than we do in the United States, they're training our kids through the Internet!" Buried somewhere in Trump's babbling rhetoric (should we really hate Iran for their Internet connections?) is a disturbing call to "bomb the hell" out of both Iraq and Iran, followed by Trump's only consistent foreign policy position: stealing oil from other countries.

Trump is always his own top adviser. In one interview, Trump was asked what experts he was consulting about foreign policy. He said: "I'm speaking with myself, number one, because I have a very good brain, and I've said a lot of things." Trump has indeed said a lot of things, but none of them indicate that he has a very good brain or should be trusted to run foreign policy. Trump would not listen to experts on foreign policy. This is a particularly dangerous approach to foreign policy because it means Trump will be locked into his first instincts.

Some naive leftists have praised Trump's foreign policy proposals, and his claims that he opposes military interventions and NATO. But Trump is a violent isolationist. This makes his foreign policy highly unpredictable. It's possible that he might not invade a particular country because he doesn't follow the advice of foreign policy elites. But he might also start lots of wars (against the advice of those same elites) because he thinks being tough is the solution to every problem. So Trump's interventions might be different from those of a more conventional candidate, but they're likely to be much greater in number.

At a March 10, 2016 Republican debate, Trump was asked if he would invade Iraq and Syria: "Mr. Trump, more troops?" Trump declared: "We really have no choice. We have to knock out ISIS. We have to knock the hell out of them. We have to get rid of it. And then come back and rebuild our country, which is falling apart. We have no choice." When asked how many troops he would send, Trump said: "I would listen to the generals, but I'm hearing numbers of 20,000 to 30,000. We have to knock them out fast."

Later that month, Trump denied that he said what he said: "I didn't say send 20,000. I said, well the generals are saying you'd need because they, what would it take to wipe out ISIS, I said pretty much exactly this, I said the generals, the military is saying you would need 20- to 30,000 troops, but I didn't say that I would send them." According to Trump, "I'd get people from that part of the world to put up the troops, and I'd certainly give them air power and air support and some military support … I would never ever put up 20,000 or 30,000." In Trump's mind, he can simply make a deal to convince other countries to invade Iraq and Syria on behalf of the United States.

Trump is one of the biggest warmongers ever to run as a major party candidate for president. No candidate, not even Barry Goldwater, has ever embraced using nuclear weapons against cities in order to kill a small terrorist force.

On *Meet the Press*, Trump proudly asserted that he would become the first person in the world to use nuclear weapons in peacetime to murder thousands of innocent civilians: "We're going to hit them and we're going to hit them hard. I'm talking about a surgical strike on these ISIS stronghold cities using Trident missiles." The Trident missile is a submarine-launched ballistic missile typically equipped with eight 100-kiloton nuclear warheads, a missile with a total of about 50 times the power of the Hiroshima nuclear bomb. Trump promised to use not just one, but multiple "Trident missiles." And "stronghold cities" are not enemy camps, but cities, places with thousands of innocent civilians where ISIS holds military control.

After the backlash to these plans, Trump backed off slightly, claiming it was "highly unlikely" he would use nuclear weapons against ISIS, but still refusing to reject the possibility: "I just don't want to talk about it." Helene Cooper of the *New York Times* spoke with Pentagon and military personnel about Trump's views on nuclear weapons and reported that "they were appalled."

Trump's approach to foreign policy is not a complete mystery. Today, Trump contradicts his past comments on Iraq and Libya and Egypt because he doesn't remember what he said before. He does not learn from his mistakes, because he always refuses to acknowledge any mistakes, and so his foreign policy will simply rely on his own instincts. And what are Trump's instincts? Based on his public comments about ISIS, Libya, and Iraq, Trump's instincts are to engage in acts of brutal, merciless violence with little regard to the consequences. Whenever faced with a threat to American interests, Trump would bomb first, steal oil second, and ask questions later.

Trump also tends to attack everything about his political opponents (indeed, the only reason why he spoke out harshly about the war in Iraq in the 2016 primary was due to his campaign battle with Jeb Bush). As a result, his 2016 campaign against Hillary Clinton will set Trump's foreign policy to contradict almost anything from Clinton and the Obama Administration. Wherever the Obama Administration stood up for human rights against repressive regimes, Trump would replace it with deal-making and appeasement or even friendship, as he has indicated with Vladimir Putin of Russia. Trump feels a kinship with dictators because they tend to share his love of ostentatious wealth and the ability to command underlings to do whatever he wants.

Some people actually believe the "Donald the Dove" act that Trump displays solely because many Americans are tired of war. In reality, Trump is extraordinarily militaristic. That's not a baseless insult; that's what Trump says about himself: "I'm the most militaristic person there is."

No one knows if a President Trump would actually fulfill his promises to launch a nuclear weapon against ISIS, to invade numerous nations, and to start various wars. It is probable that Trump would be a diplomatic disaster, almost certain to alienate American allies and enemies alike. But because Trump lies about everything and contradicts himself on a daily basis, it is also entirely possible that as president he would become distracted by installing gold-plated amenities around the White House and by making sure that Trump Water is stocked in the fridge, never quite getting around to starting any of the military actions he has promised. But it's also possible Trump would be even more militaristic than he claims, launching attacks in unexpected places due to his conspiratorial thinking, his poor judgment, his complete ignorance, and his propensity for vengeance.

TRUMP'S LIES ABOUT HILLARY CLINTON

Trump has called Hillary Clinton "a world-class liar." Politifact rated 71 percent of statements made by Donald Trump to be false (compared to 29 percent by Clinton), and 18 percent of Trump's untruths were rated "pants on fire" lies, compared to only 2 percent of Clinton's statements. Factcheck.org noted about Trump, "In the 12 years of FactCheck.org's existence, we've never seen his match. He stands out not only for the sheer number of his factually false claims, but also for his brazen refusals to admit error when proven wrong."

In 2012, with more than three out of her four years as Secretary of State completed, Trump declared his admiration for Hillary Clinton: "Hillary Clinton, I think, is a terrific woman. I mean, I'm a little biased because I've known her for years. I live in New York. She lives in New York. And I've known her and her husband for years and I really like 'em both a lot and I think she really works hard and I think she, again, she's given an agenda that's not all of her, but I think she really works hard, and I think she does a good job. And I like her."

Trump now claims that "Hillary Clinton's agenda" is to "release the violent criminals from jail. She wants them all released." Only a lunatic would imagine that Clinton has ever proposed this idea. Trump makes all kinds of wild accusations against Clinton that have no basis in fact: "Hillary is going to ban fracking. Hillary is going to abolish the Second Amendment."

According to Trump, "She ran the State Department like her own personal hedge fund—doing favors for oppressive regimes, and really, many, many others, in exchange for cash. Pure and simple, folks, pure and simple." Despite the lack of evidence supporting these claims, Trump assumed that Clinton was engaged in bribery because that's what Trump does: "I've got to give to them, because when I want something, I get it. When I call, they kiss my ass."

One of the attacks Trump made against Hillary Clinton was the idea that she lacks the "stamina" to be president. To prove that, Trump summoned the ghost of Benghazi, "Among the victims is our late Ambassador, Chris Stevens. He was left helpless to die as Hillary Clinton soundly slept in her bed—that's right, when the phone rang at 3 o'clock in the morning, she was sleeping." In reality, the first alert was sent at 3:45 pm, and Clinton wasn't sleeping (although if she had been sleeping at 3 am, that would hardly qualify as a lack of stamina or failure to do her job).

Trump explained that he didn't actually know if his statement was true: "she was asleep at the wheel. Whether she was sleeping or not, who knows if she was sleeping." Trump concluded, "Whether she was sleeping or not, and she might have been sleeping, it was a disaster." To Trump, the literal truth doesn't matter. If something feels true to him, if it's metaphorically true, and if he thinks it might be true, then the actual truth is unimportant. In fact, even when the real facts are given to him, he still believes he "might" have been correct in his false smear.

Trump's casual relationship with the truth makes him an extraordinary political figure. It's difficult to name any presidential candidate who has ever lied more consistently than Trump, and with such indifference to the truth.

MANIPULATING THE MINIMUM WAGE

Perhaps Trump does have a "first rate mind," as F. Scott Fitzgerald would define it. For Trump, it's easy to hold two contradictory positions simultaneously because he doesn't have an ideology. On raising the minimum wage, Trump repeatedly expressed his opposition to it during most of the Republican primary. In August 2015, Trump said, "Having a low minimum wage is not a bad thing for this country." During a Republican debate in Milwaukee in November 2015, Trump said about increasing the minimum wage, "I would not do it" and that "Taxes too high, wages too high, we're not going to be able to compete against the world." A month later, when Bernie Sanders repeated what Trump said, Trump tweeted that Sanders "said that I feel wages in America are too high. Lie!" But it was Trump who lied, mainly because he paid no attention to what he said.

In 2016 Trump suddenly reversed course and said he might support a minimum wage increase: "I'm actually looking at that because I am very different from most Republicans. You have to have something that you can live on." For Trump's working-class base, a minimum wage increase was strongly desired, even if it didn't fit with Republican policies.

Ultimately, Trump decided to simultaneously support and oppose a higher minimum wage. On May 8, 2016, Trump was asked about the federal minimum wage on two Sunday morning shows. On ABC's *This Week* he announced, "I think people have to get more" and then on *Meet the Press* he declared his opposition to any federal minimum wage: "I would say let the states decide." Of course, letting the states decide the minimum wage means abolishing the federal minimum wage. So on May 11, Elizabeth Warren tweeted: "You care so much about struggling American workers, @realDonaldTrump, that you want to abolish the federal minimum wage?" Later that day, Trump tweeted back: "Goofy Elizabeth Warren lied when she says I want to abolish the Federal Minimum Wage. See media—asking for increase!"

After Bernie Sanders pointed out that Trump had called for abolishing the federal minimum wage, Trump said "Bernie Sanders lied," and Trump claimed, "Every factchecker said Trump never said that." In reality, that very same day Politifact had rated Sanders' claim about Trump "Mostly True" and pointed out that Trump's incoherent and contradictory statements were the only reason why it wasn't rated completely true.

Then Trump announced that he would support an increase in the federal minimum wage to $10 an hour. Stephen Moore, a Heritage Foundation economist advising the Trump campaign on economic issues, said: "The $10 minimum wage, that was the first I'd heard of that …Sometimes he says one thing, and sometimes he says another about this, so I'm not exactly sure where he's at on this."

Trump has (sometimes simultaneously) called for freezing the federal minimum wage, abolishing the minimum wage, and increasing it by 38 percent. No one in the history of politics has ever taken so many radically different positions on the minimum wage as Trump managed to do within a few months. So which position does he truly believe in? Trump believes in nothing except pandering to any political position he thinks will help him win.

TRUMPONOMICS

As a businessman, Trump touts his economic expertise, but it is remarkable how little he understands. Trump repeatedly claims, "We are the highest-taxed nation in the world." In reality, the US tax burden is one of the lowest in the industrialized world, ranking lower than nearly all of the 34 countries in the Organization for Economic Cooperation and Development, with only Chile, South Korea, and Mexico having a lower tax rate. Taxes were 26 percent of the total U.S. economy in 2014, far below Germany (36.1) or Sweden (42.7).

Trump has also promised to completely solve America's debt problem: "We've got to get rid of the $19 trillion in debt." When the *Washington Post* asked him: "How long would that take?" Trump answered: "I would say over a period of eight years."

This idea was so crazy that Trump was forced to backtrack. *Fortune* magazine asked him about paying off the national debt within ten years, and Trump denied ever saying it: "No, I didn't say ten years." (Technically, Trump is right—he said eight years, not ten.) Trump then said about the national debt, "You could pay off a percentage of it" within ten years. Even that promise would be impossible for Trump to keep. Trump has proposed a massive tax cut, huge increases in spending on the military and infrastructure, and no cuts for any entitlements. It's almost mathematically impossible for Trump to reduce the deficit under his plans, and running surpluses that would reduce the national debt is completely inconceivable if Trump keeps any of his promises. Trump claimed that he would be able to do it because "I'm renegotiating all of our deals" on trade. But even if Trump somehow managed to get "better" trade deals, the likely effect would be to slightly increase jobs in America offset by higher costs for consumers. There would be no massive payoff to the US government that would reduce the debt.

Trump once proposed a 14.25 percent tax on the net worth of the wealthy to raise $6 trillion and wipe out the national debt, which would have been the largest tax hike in the history of the world. Now he's proposing massive tax cuts on the rich that would cause the debt to hit record highs. An analysis by the nonpartisan Tax Policy Center, and confirmed by Citizens for Tax Justice, found that under Donald Trump's tax plan, the top 0.1 percent of taxpayers would get more overall tax relief than the bottom 60 percent of taxpayers combined. For the highest income earners, the top income tax rate would drop from 39.6 percent to 25 percent. The top 0.1 percent of taxpayers, with an income over $3.7 million per year, would get an average tax cut of more than $1.3 million every year under Trump's plan.

In 1999, Trump considered a run on the ticket of Ross Perot's Reform Party, and wanted to appeal to a broad range of the electorate, emphasizing fiscal responsibility. But when Trump planned to run in the Republican primary, a communist plan to confiscate wealth would cost him votes, so it was replaced with a massive tax cut for the rich. Which plan does Trump believe in? Obviously, the plan that cuts Trump's own taxes is closer to his heart, but the fact that he could seriously propose a massive wealth tax shows that Trump is willing to say anything to get elected, because he believes in nothing. Trump's approach to tax cuts allows him to pose as a populist while still pursuing his goal of cutting taxes on the wealthiest people like himself. Trump announced that under his plan, the rich would "pay more." But what he meant was something very different: "If I increase it on the wealthy, that means they're still going to be paying less than they're paying now. . . . I'm talking about increasing from my tax proposal," which would cut the top tax rate from 39.6 percent to 25 percent. Trump could simultaneously appeal to conservatives who wanted to cut taxes on the rich and the working-class voters who resented growing inequality and wanted the rich to pay more.

A Trump presidency would be disastrous to the economy and would be almost certain to cause massive increases in the national debt because of these enormous tax cuts for the wealthy. A Moody's analytic team determined that Trump's economic proposals would be a disaster for America: "Under the scenario in which all of his stated policies become law in the manner proposed, the economy suffers a lengthy recession and is smaller at the end of his four-year term than when he took office. By the end of his presidency, there are closer to 3.5 million fewer jobs and the unemployment rate rises to as high as 7 percent, compared with below 5 percent today. During Mr. Trump's presidency, the average American household's after-inflation income will stagnate, and stock prices and real house values will decline."

Some people might imagine that because Trump is opposed by the political establishment, that he will therefore serve the interests of the working class who feel disenfranchised. But not everything in economics is a zero-sum game. Sometimes, an economic plan is bad for almost everybody. Because Trump doesn't actually have a political ideology, his economic plans have no coherent approach.

THE MEMORY HOLE OF DONALD TRUMP

Amazingly, Trump claims that he is unusual because of his truth-telling: "I have a nasty habit that most career politicians don't have:

I tell the truth. I'm not afraid to say exactly what I believe. When I'm asked a question, I don't answer with a speech that ignores a controversial subject. I answer the question."

In fact, Trump rarely ever answers a question. An entire book could be filled with the numerous instances where Trump has ignored a question he doesn't like and had instead digressed about a completely different subject. Trump isn't honest; but he is forthright. He's happy to say offensive things about his opponents, his critics, Mexicans, Muslims, women, and almost anybody else who wanders into range of his hateful tirades. Trump has confused speaking his mind with telling the truth.

Incredibly, Trump keeps creating new controversies that obscure the old ones. Trump's flurry of misinformation prevents anyone from focusing on any individual error for very long. When every outrage is followed by another outrage, it becomes difficult to remember the long list of Trump's errors and deceptions.

In an interview with the *New York Times*, Trump promised, "I would tax China coming in—products coming in. I would do a tariff . . . . The tax should be 45 percent." When the *Times* reported this fact, Trump simply denied saying what he was recorded saying: "That's wrong. They were wrong. It's the *New York Times*. They're always wrong."

Trump even lies about lying. The morning after the Feb. 13, 2016 Republican debate, Trump claimed: "I didn't call anybody a liar." But everybody saw him tell Ted Cruz at the debate, "You are the single biggest liar. This guy lied—let me just tell you, this guy lied about Ben Carson . . . . That's a lot of lies."

Trump's exaggerations and outright deceptions are extraordinary. No one tells lies bigger and better than Donald Trump. He has the best lies.

2 BANKRUPT TRUMP

Trump's claim that he is qualified to be president rests almost entirely upon his wealth. Trump is famous for being rich, and rich for being famous. He survived a series of terrible financial decisions in the early 1990s, but only because of his celebrity status, barely escaped bankruptcy. And since then, he has become enormously wealthy because he is a celebrity star who has turned that fame into a lucrative brand name. This fact particularly undercuts the idea that Trump's economic success qualifies him to be president. If the federal budget could be balanced by licensing the brand name of "America" to foreign buildings, then Trump could make a claim to be a qualified leader.

According to Trump, "There's a big difference between creating wealth and being a member of the lucky sperm club." But Trump never really created wealth; he was just an outlet for very rich people to waste their money on overvalued real estate. And no one has had luckier sperm than Trump. Trump didn't just grow up rich, with millions as a guaranteed inheritance and a family chauffeur to drive him around in the Trump limo. He also had the good fortune to grow up as part of a politically-connected real estate empire in New York City, and at a time when Manhattan property was dramatically undervalued.

Trump didn't plan any of this. He simply wanted to be famous. After toying with the idea of going to film school in California and becoming a Hollywood producer, he wisely decided to stick with the family business in real estate. But unlike his conservative father, who got rich building subsidized public housing in the outer boroughs, Trump wanted to be part of New York celebrity's life. That meant he needed to do big deals in Manhattan.

Trump's first major development was the Grand Hyatt Hotel in midtown Manhattan, but the deal only happened because of a New York City tax subsidy worth $400 million over 40 years. This enormous and unprecedented tax abatement, the first ever for a commercial property in New York City, was made possible with the help of his father's influential political allies. Fred Trump's gifts to his son included his money, his real estate savvy, and his knowledge of how to operate in a corrupt political system and turn it into massive profits.

According to Trump, "The working man likes me because he knows I didn't inherit what I've built." But he certainly didn't make his money appealing to the working man: Trump based his real estate empire on appealing to the very rich, which turned out to be a highly successful strategy when growing inequality produced massive increases in the wealth of the richest people.

Trump would have lost his wealth and gone bankrupt in the 1990s if not for the value of his celebrity name. He was too big to fail, and so bankers thought they had to bail him out because his name brand was the biggest asset he had when he was hundreds of millions of dollars in debt.

THE SELF-MADE TRUMP

Trump is a self-created image of a great businessman. Trump claimed, "The money I've earned was the result of my own work." That's not true. Trump's money has also come from his father's business and from public subsidies, while many others have been forced to bear the losses on his risky investments that failed.

Trump portrays himself as a self-made man: "I earned every penny. When I was beginning my career my father never gave me much money, but gave me a great work ethic." Trump wrote about his father, "He loaned me a small amount of money—loaned, not gave—around $1 million." It's difficult to imagine any average American being able to ask their father for a $1 million loan— or considering a million dollars a "small amount of money." Trump's first real estate investments were also co-signed by his father, which was the only way an unknown could get huge bank loans. Trump got another $7.5 million loan from his father to buy land in Atlantic City. And then, when Trump faced dire financial problem, his father bought $3.5 million in chips from Trump

Castle without using them—effectively giving his son a low-risk loan that was later deemed illicit by the gaming commission. Trump also used his father's estate as collateral to get a $10 million loan from his siblings.

Trump bought the Castle in 1985 without ever stepping inside it. He had no experience managing a casino, had no experienced managers, and paid $320 million with a $280 million personally guaranteed loan. Trump lied to regulators, telling them he would borrow money at low interest rates, but he was forced to pay such high interest rates that his casinos were almost guaranteed to fail, even if Trump had been competent at running them (which he wasn't).

By the late 1980s, Mr. Trump's holdings included three casinos, the Plaza Hotel in New York, the nearby Trump Tower, and the Trump Shuttle airline. He was buried in debt, and Trump noted, "I watched my empire collapsing."

In 1991, the Taj Mahal went bankrupt, followed by Trump Castle and Trump Plaza in 1992. Other casinos in Atlantic City Trump Entertainment Resorts—his casino business—went bankrupt twice, and he lost money every year from 1995 to 2009, except for 2005.

The Trump ethic is to screw over everybody else. In the wake of Trump's financial success is a long list of people who suffered from his poor decisions: employees laid off, vendors who went unpaid, bondholders who lost money, and stockholders who watched their investments disappear under Trump's highly-paid management. At the Taj Mahal, Trump forced contractors to take at least a 30 percent cut in what they were owed, and he felt no guilt about doing it: "They made plenty of money on me." According to a report, "One contractor, who spoke on the condition of anonymity for fear of being sued by Mr. Trump, said Mr. Trump underpaid on one large job, at one of his towers, by almost $100,000."

Trump noted that one of the ways he makes money is by refusing to pay contractors what he owes them, and occasionally won't pay fully when the work is simply satisfactory or "an OK to bad job...If it's OK, then I'll sometimes cut them." In dealing with public projects such as building bridges, Trump claimed, "that should be the attitude of the country." But these tricks don't work: contractors simply inflate their prices to account for attempted discounts if they know the person they are dealing with is unscrupulous. Trump's approach would be an invitation for more political corruption: politically connected contractors would lobby their friends in the government or Congress to ensure they received full payment.

Trump's modus operandi is to get rich by making his companies pay him for the privilege of running them into bankruptcy. At the Taj Mahal, Trump bought voting control over the public company, and then gave himself a service contract for $108 million over five years to run the company. Then he took a $60 million payoff to terminate the service contract when the Taj Mahal was failing before it even opened.

The *New York Times* reported, "Trump pulled more than $1 million from his failing public company, describing the transaction in securities filings in ways that may have been illegal, according to legal experts."

Wayne Barrett noted, "all of the financials that he gave the banks were totally false." Trump could have faced not just personal bankruptcy, but also criminal charges for his fraud. In 2002, federal securities regulators issued a cease and desist order against the company, saying it had misled shareholders by publishing a news release with numbers "deceptively" skewed.

THE BEGGAR AND THE BILLIONAIRE

In his 1997 book, *The Art of the Comeback*, Trump recounts telling Marla Maples as they passed by a beggar, "He's a beggar, but he's worth about $900 million more than me." In his 2004 book, *How to Get Rich*, Trump writes, "In the midst of the crash, I passed a beggar on the street and realized he was worth $9.2 billion more than I was." By his 2007 book *Think Big and Kick Ass in Business and Life*, the beggar was back to $900 million. How could Trump give two such wildly different figures when reciting the same story?

Trump admitted that the $9.2 billion figure "is a mistake, and I don't know how it got there." He explained, "whether it's $9 billion or $3.6 billion, I don't think makes any difference to anybody if they hear the story."

Trump admitted, "I'd personally guaranteed a billion dollars. I was a schmuck, but I was a lucky schmuck..." This is the man claiming that his financial genius qualifies him to help run the world economy: "a lucky schmuck." The capitalist system is designed to make foolish, reckless people very wealthy with no threat to their personal fortune as long as they can find a banker dumb enough to loan them money. Trump took a system rigged completely in his favor and came within an inch of losing all of his buildings, as well as his entire personal fortune of hundreds of millions of dollar and his reputation as a great businessman with a celebrity brand.

Business acumen and personal genius had little to do with Trump's survival, as he readily acknowledges. Trump went to the banks and threatened them: "I can tie you guys up for years—in court proceedings, bankruptcy filings, and the other legal maneuvers I'm good at—when forced." He offered not to sue them for $65 million in loans. Trump bragged that if they hadn't given in to him, the banks would have faced "one of the most complicated proceedings ever" that would cost them "vast amounts of time and money."

Trump was saved by government regulation. Because he had a casino license and his creditors didn't, they needed him to stay involved. Reporter David Cay Johnston noted, "the only reason Donald is a viable candidate today is that in 1990, when he couldn't pay his bills even though he claimed to be a billionaire, the state of New Jersey Casino Control Commission took his side against his bankers. So it was government intervention in the market that saved him." The commission allowed him to keep his gaming licenses because "he was too big to fail," said a former commission chairman.

Trump emphasizes the importance of his "hard work." One time, he explains, when he was deeply in debt, he didn't want to go to a bankers' dinner, but he did the "hard work" of showing up. His most hostile banker happened to be sitting next to him at the event, and "wanted to talk about women." After Trump charmed him, the banker made a deal with him. Trump says, "I got very lucky" and it probably saved him from bankruptcy. According to Trump, "That one event changed the course of my life."

In addition to bragging about his sexual prowess with women, Trump also used golf to impress bankers. After playing golf with one banker and helping him improve his golf game, Trump reported, "hundreds of millions of dollars' worth of problems went away. Just like that. Pfff!"

Much of Trump's success came from the skillful use of the threat of bankruptcy: "I settled the liens for a small fraction of the face amount...." Because Trump's name brand had been built into the valuation of the company, the banks were better off with Trump's association.

One of Trump's bankers explained, "However absurd this sounds, it was smarter to do it this way than to let a judge preside over a fire sale in a bankruptcy court." That's because what little value a Trump casino had was Trump himself. He held the casino license, and he had the celebrity brand. Trump was too big to fail. With the help of his friendly and desperate bankers, Trump was given $65 million and enough time to stave off personal bankruptcy.

Trump was still deep in personal debt and holding bad investments in his Atlantic City casinos. By the mid-1990s, Trump's terrible financial history made him too much of a risk for most bankers. But he found new suckers willing to give him money based on his exaggerated celebrity status: shareholders.

LOSING STOCK IN TRUMP

In 1995, Trump took one of his companies public and raised $140 million in investments. Trump then used the public company to enrich himself at the expense of stockholders. He took the money to pay off the debts for which Trump himself was personally liable. Then Trump sold his two worst debt-ridden assets, the Trump Taj Mahal and the Trump Castle, to his own public company at inflated prices. Trump's company bought the Trump Castle from Trump for $100 million more than analysts said it was worth, and then Trump paid himself an extra $880,000 for arranging the whole thing. The company's stock price plummeted immediately.

Graef Crystal, an executive-pay consultant, noted: "He ran these companies into the ground." Trump decided to load up his casinos with debt and take the money for his own use: "I said: 'OK. Now it's junk-bond time. It's been a great experience, but I'm out.'" As Trump noted, "The Taj Mahal was a very successful job for me. It's not personal. This was just business. I got out great."

Trump took companies that he controlled, and had them sign contracts with him to pay him millions and millions of dollars in management fees while he was mismanaging them and running up debts. Trump was a financial vampire, gradually sucking the life out of his victims to pay off his debts.

Trump's creditors allowed him to make money from bankrupting his companies, sometimes literally. In 1992, Trump Casino paid Trump $1.5 million to guide it through bankruptcy. When Trump Hotels and Casinos Resorts went bankrupt, the reorganization plan gave Trump $2 million a year plus expenses to run the company he had driven into the ground, plus a minority stake in the Miss Universe pageant. From 1990 to 1996, Trump made more than $160 million in fees and payouts from his Atlantic City casinos, all while he was gutting them. Trump bragged, "For many years I took money out of Atlantic City. The money I made in Atlantic City fueled a lot of projects."

Trump used the public company as his personal expense account to maintain his lavish lifestyle, spending $6 million entertaining high-end customers and $2 million in company money to maintain his personal jet and pilots. Trump also used his power over the public company to purchase Trump products from a privately-owned Trump corporation, including $1.2 million worth of Trump Ice bottled water between 2006 and 2009.

From 1995 to 2005, the value of the Trump company's stock dropped 96% and was then delisted as the company went bankrupt. But Trump got rich bankrupting his own company. In 2004,

Trump praised the stock offering: "Entrepreneurially speaking, not necessarily from the standpoint of running a company but from an entrepreneur's standpoint, it was one of the great deals." It was a great deal for the entrepreneur Trump: he made massive profits from pillaging the company for his personal gain, profiting from hundreds of millions of dollars in salary, benefits, expenses, and personal debt erased.

Trump kept close control over the company, even putting his 26-year-old daughter Ivanka on the Board of Directors in 2007 with a six-figure salary. By 2009, Trump dropped out of the company, because the stock was completely worthless.

THE ART OF THE FAILURE

To Trump, even his failure as a businessman became evidence of his success. In 2004, Trump Hotels & Casinos finished a bankruptcy reorganization, removing $500 million of its $1.8 billion in debt. Trump declared, "I don't think it's a failure, it's a success."

Being nearly a billion dollar in debt and on the verge of bankruptcy was a sign of his greatness because he managed to overcome it all. Failure only expanded Trump's brand name: He added "the art of the comeback" to his "art of the deal" shtick. He became more relatable to the average person because he could point to difficulties in his own past. Trump explained that his business failures were a result of being "distracted" by his celebrity status and "taking his eye off the ball," so they weren't really the product of his ideas and abilities.

In 1990, Trump blamed his failure on too much easy success: "I made a lot of money and I made it too easily, to the point of boredom. Anything I did worked! I took on Bally, I made $32 million. After a while it was too easy." Total failure didn't make Trump modest; it made him more arrogant than ever. He believed his only flaw was that he was too good and made too much money, and that caused him to be distracted. The lesson Trump learned was that if he just paid attention, then he couldn't fail.

The kind of tactics Trump used to escape financial ruin, sending his companies into bankruptcy and using the threat of bankruptcy to reduce his debt, would be catastrophic for the United States, where even the hint of such a possibility would send the global economy into a recession.

TRUMP'S MOB CONNECTIONS

Trump has very strong mob connections. Trump's mentor, Roy Cohn, was a lawyer for the two top Mafia families in New York, including the Genovese family led by "Fat Tony" Salerno and the Gambino family, led by Paul Castellano. Trump reportedly met with Salerno at Cohn's townhouse.

Salerno and Castellano also ran S&A Concrete, and controlled the ready-mix concrete business in New York, which Trump used to build Trump Plaza. A federal indictment of Salerno which sent him to prison concluded that Trump had paid inflated prices for his concrete. Why would Trump, the man who claimed to be the greatest at making deals, overpay millions for concrete?

The indictment on which Salerno was convicted in 1988 and sent to prison, where he died, listed the nearly $8 million contract for concrete at Trump Plaza, an East Side high-rise apartment building, as one of the acts establishing that S&A was part of a racketeering enterprise. The mob connections also meant that Trump could avoid having a picket line despite using nonunion workers.

Cohn was also a friend of John Cody, the mob-connected leader of Teamsters Local 282, who knew Trump well, although Trump called him "a very bad cookie." When Cody ordered a citywide strike, the work continued at Trump Tower. Cody had previously obtained free apartments from other developers as a kickback, and Cody's girlfriend, despite having no job, acquired three apartments in Trump Tower underneath Trump's own apartment. Trump helped her get a $3 million mortgage without filling out a loan application.

After Cody was imprisoned and lost control of the union, Trump turned against Cody's girlfriend, suing her for $250,000. She promptly countersued for $20 million and accused Trump of kickbacks that could result in a "criminal proceeding." Trump, who claims (incorrectly) that he never settles lawsuits, settled with her for $500,000. Why would Trump suddenly give a woman $500,000 after trying to sue her for $250,000? Might Trump have been trying to keep a potential witness quiet who might endanger his business, or even cause him problems with the Justice Department?

Trump's first licensing deal in 1988 was with a mob-connected friend, John Staluppi of the Colombo crime family, who owned Dillinger Coach Works (named for the famous mobster) and who worked with Trump to create Trump Executive Series stretch limousines. Felix Sater, a senior Trump advisor and son of a reputed Russian mobster, was kept on by Trump long after he was convicted in a mob-connected stock swindle.

One of Trump's friends was a major narcotics dealer named Joseph Weichselbaum, who ran a company that provided helicopter service for Trump and the high rollers at his casinos. Weichselbaum pled guilty to federal cocaine distribution and income tax charges, and had a felony record that included grand theft auto and embezzlement. For Weichselbaum's sentencing hearing, Trump wrote a letter praising the drug trafficker as "conscientious, forthright, and diligent" and "a credit to the community." Shortly after Weichselbaum was indicted, Trump personally rented him an apartment in Trump Plaza. While Weichselbaum was serving three years in prison, his girlfriend bought two multi-million-dollar apartments in Trump Tower, where Weichselbaum later lived as an ex-con after seeking early release with the promise that Trump had a job waiting for him.

Trump and his casinos were also closely linked with Robert LiButti, who was eventually banned by state gaming officials from Atlantic City casinos because of his mob connections. Trump Plaza was fined $200,000 because Trump's casino repeatedly removed African-American and female dealers from LiButti's craps table as he demanded. Trump's casino was also fined $450,000 for giving LiButti millions of dollars in gifts.

In 1991, Trump claimed about LiButti, "I wouldn't know what he looked like," and in 2016 Trump asserted, "I don't recognize the name." By contrast, LiButti has said: "I'm very close with him." LiButti frequently rode in Trump's helicopter with Trump's wife and children. Trump attended LiButti's daughter's birthday party at Trump Plaza, and joined them on Trump's yacht. Trump even negotiated with LiButti to buy a racing horse from him for $500,000 until the horse went lame from an illness.

TRUMP'S BILLIONS

Is Trump exaggerating his wealth? Of course he is. For a man whose primary vocabulary runs from "huge" to "tremendous," exaggeration is constant. Trump always exaggerates his assets, unless he's trying to avoid taxes. (Jack Blum, chairman of the Tax Justice Network, has called Trump a "poster child" for tax avoidance property schemes.)

In a deposition, Trump was asked if he would ever inflate the value of his properties in his statements, and he answered, "Not beyond reason." In another deposition, Trump explained that he raised the value of one property from $80 million in 2005 to $150 million in 2006 based on his personal opinion alone. Trump also explained: "My net worth fluctuates, and it goes up and down with the markets and with attitudes and with feelings, even my own feelings."

Asked in the deposition about his statements in 2007 that his net worth was $8 billion, Trump conceded: "I don't know. I don't think so. Well, maybe I'm adding four or five billion dollars worth, three billion, for the value of a brand. But I don't know." In 2011, Trump printed a financial statement in one of his books estimating his net worth at just over $7 billion, of which $3 billion (over 42%) consisted of his "brand value."

But make no mistake: Trump is incredibly, unbelievably wealthy. It's probably not $10 billion, as he claims. Yet Trump is certainly a billionaire. And that is Trump's primary claim to fame, and his key qualification to be president. The theory Trump presents to the public is that his extraordinary wealth is evidence of extraordinary skills that he could use as president to greatly improve the United States.

However, Trump got rich because of a mixture of inheritance, luck, celebrity status, real estate savvy, and heavy risk-taking while making others pay for his bad deals. Far from being evidence of his qualifications to be a good president, Trump's manner of gaining wealth reveals a path with little relevance to excelling as leader of the free world. Worst of all, Trump's arrogance—his belief that his money proves his greatness—makes him vulnerable to terrible errors in judgment and blunders. A man who thinks he never makes a mistake will never learn from his mistakes.

TRUMP'S ILLEGAL IMMIGRANTS

Trump has made the war on illegal immigrants his signature issue. But Trump himself has used illegal immigrants. Trump's contractor hired illegal immigrants from Poland to do the demolition work for the site of the Trump Tower, paying them $4 an hour and then failing to give them the money they earned. Trump's employees threatened the immigrants with deportation if they caused trouble. And Trump knew all about the problem. Two workers testified that they approached Trump in person to demand wages that hadn't been paid to them. Despite the clear-cut evidence and litigation, Trump claimed, "Nobody's proven to me that they were illegal." And yet Trump went to Daniel Sullivan, a labor fixer and FBI informant, who testified: "Donald told me that he was having his difficulties and he admitted to me that—seeking my advice—that he had some illegal Polish employees on the job. I reacted by saying to Donald that 'I think you are nuts.' I told him to fire them promptly if he had any brains." Trump knowingly employed illegal immigrants, lied about the fact, and then refused to pay them. When the immigrants filed a lawsuit against Trump, the faux-Trump "John Baron" called up their lawyer, threatening to sue him for $100 million unless he dropped the suit.

Trump's Mar-a-Lago Club hired only 17 out of 300 Americans who applied for jobs, using special business visas instead to bring in foreign workers. Trump claimed, "you could not get people" in America to take the jobs. In July 2016, the Mar-a-Lago Club and Trump National Golf Club filed temporary visa applications for 78 positions for servers, housekeepers, and cooks, even though a local job placement agency reported that it had a database of more than 1300 Americans seeking these hospitality jobs and Trump's company had never contacted them to find workers.

Trump's hypocrisy also includes his trade policy. While Trump declared that "China is raping this country," virtually all of the Donald J. Trump Signature Collection is made overseas, much of it in China. According to Trump, "They don't even make this stuff here." Either Trump was intentionally lying, or he cared so little about American workers that he never even bothered to consider making his products in the US (with the exception of his "Make America Great Again" hats). Trump wrote that he was forced to make his products overseas: "I'm a realist. I'm a competitor."

At an event with Chris Christie, Trump announced: "I'm not eating Oreos anymore, you know that—but neither is Chris. You're not eating Oreos anymore." There's nothing necessarily hypocritical about a businessman who makes his products in other countries but calls for changes in trade policies. But it's completely hypocritical for Trump to make his ties in China because labor is cheap and then promise that he's "never eating another Oreo again" because another company uses the same logic.

Trump repeatedly claims that currency manipulation is the cause of the trade deficit with China, but the real reason is the gap in wages. That's why Trump makes some of his products in some low-wage countries other than China. It's also why Trump's plan for a trade war with China won't succeed: manufacturers will simply move production to a different low-wage country, as many of them are already doing because wages in China are starting to rise.

The trade issue also shows the limits of thinking that expertise in business translates to expertise in politics. Trump understands trade enough to move his production to other countries. But because Trump doesn't really understand international trade, he seizes upon "currency manipulation" as the only reason why manufacturing jobs are leaving the United States.

THE LUCK OF TRUMP

As Trump himself acknowledges, the word that describes much of his business career is "lucky." He was lucky to be born at the right time so that he could enter the Manhattan real estate market at a down time, when it was ready to explode in value. He was lucky to escape from his bad casino investments without losing his entire fortune. And he has been remarkably lucky that none of his business errors or offensive comments have ever tarnished the luxury brand name that is the core of his entire business enterprise. Trump didn't get rich by being a business genius. He got rich, and stayed rich, by being Trump—by being a celebrity businessman famous for being famous.

Trump inherited his fortune and his real estate connections. But he used his inheritance to forge a new direction for the family company, one that was aimed at the heart of Manhattan and had the goal of turning himself into a global celebrity.

In all of this, Trump never really had a business scheme in mind. He just wanted to be famous. He never imagined that becoming famous could be a business tactic, that instead of paying money to put his name on buildings, rich foreigners would come to him asking to give him money in exchange for having his name on the marquee. Trump's entire business model was an accidental byproduct of his narcissistic desire to be famous.

In real estate development and the art of the deal, Trump had occasional success (much of it due to his inheritance of the family business) and some devastating failures. It's only in the art of being a celebrity that Trump is a true genius and an unqualified success.

Even in the one area where Trump is deemed a business success, real estate, Trump isn't an expert, he's an idiot. Trump's terrible judgment on real estate was revealed in his 2007 book, when Trump responded to a question about when was the best time to buy real estate by declaring, "Right now! . . . This is now a great time." The Trump University wealth seminars around the same time were giving similar advice to gullible Trump fans. Even when the bubble started to burst in 2007, Trump predicted that the downturn in the housing market would be "very minor" and encouraged people to buy subprime mortgages, which were the worst possible investments and the very ones that brought the economy crashing down.

Trump's understanding of the real estate market was absolutely wrong. The real estate market was at the height of the bubble that was about to burst and cause a global recession. Fortunately for Trump, he was primarily in the branding business rather than the real estate business, so the recession didn't harm him greatly.

But the real estate bubble did harm a lot of people who listened to Trump. The Trump Ocean Resort in Baja, complete with the smiling face of Donald Trump on its pamphlets, took in $32.5 million in deposits from gullible people who believed in the Trump name. Trump promised that the resort was "going to be the most spectacular place in all of Mexico." Trump personally signed an August 2007 letter to condo buyers that identified him as one of the developers. But Trump was secretly only renting out his brand to the real developers, who decided to shut down the project in 2009 without giving back any of the deposits.

One woman who lost her life savings making a deposit was recorded at a VIP reception for the project held by Ivanka Trump. The woman declared, "The Trump name is synonymous with quality." At another promotional event, Donald Trump Jr. declared that he was buying a unit at the project, but that never happened.

Trump's business has always done well in an era of growing inequality. As the rich have gotten richer over the past 35 years, Trump's high-end condos and golf resorts have done better and better. But Trump didn't recognize a business opportunity. He simply wanted to be famous, and got lucky to be born at a time when New York City had low real estate prices just at the moment he wanted to go off on his own into Manhattan. Then he built projects aimed at the very rich during the midst of a massive increase in global inequality that began during the Reagan Administration. When the rich get richer, people who make products for the very rich tend to prosper. Trump rebelled against his father's affordable housing by building unaffordable housing.

That's why Trump moved from skyscrapers to casinos to golf clubs, and why he insists upon the fanciest restaurants in his towers—without them, Trump has no way to meet the rich and powerful. Casinos offered glamour, and an opportunity to name-drop celebrities. But too few states allow casinos, and casinos are too democratic, allowing anyone in their doors. Trump wanted something more exclusive and elitist, and so he turned to private golf clubs.

TRUMP'S BRIBERY

Trump has a long record of being a political insider, constantly asking politicians (including presidents) for political favors and regularly sucking up to them. Incredibly, Trump tries to spin his corrupt political past into evidence that he's a reformer. Because he has spent most of his life bribing politicians, Trump argues that it gives him a special insight into fighting corruption.

Trump didn't just inherit his father's political contacts. Trump cultivated political influence by handing out large sums of money. In one year, Trump gave $150,000 to local candidates, and state officials said Trump circumvented state limits on political donations.

Trump is quite open about his long history of bribing public officials for political favors. When Trump encountered an honest person, such as Ned Eichler, who was in charge of deciding the fate of the Penn Central rail yards that Trump wanted, and who sent back the gifts Trump tried to bribe him with, Trump declared: "I don't know how to deal with you, Eichler, anybody else in your position would have $10 million in a cigar box tucked away." It's possible that Trump made a deal to bribe the attorney for Penn Central stockholders, agreeing to have Trump join the lawyer's lawsuit against oil companies for price-fixing in exchange for supporting his plan, although a federal probe didn't find enough evidence of wrongdoing for any indictments.

Trump said of Hugh Carey when he was running for governor of New York, "He'll do anything for a developer who gives him a campaign contribution." The Trump family donated $135,000 to help Carey win.

But the clearest evidence of Trump's bribery comes from the stories he tells in his books. Trump donated money to New York governor Mario Cuomo, and then asked him to get a political favor for Trump from his son Andrew, who was then federal Secretary of Housing and Urban Development. When Cuomo said, correctly, that it would be inappropriate, Trump proudly described how he responded: "I began screaming. 'You son of a bitch! For years I've helped you and never asked for a thing, and when I finally need something, and a totally proper thing at that, you aren't there for me. You're no good. You're one of the most disloyal people I've known and as far as I'm concerned, you can go to hell.'" To Trump, an honest politician is worse than one who is "disloyal" to him.

TRUMP'S GAS

Trump's 2011 book began with a diatribe blaming Barack Obama for five-dollar-a-gallon gas prices, which Trump saw as one of the most crucial issues facing America: "In the first two years of the Obama administration, gas prices leapt a shocking 104 percent." Trump predicted that gas prices would reach eight dollars a gallon. By 2016, gas prices had plummeted to near-record lows, but Trump was not giving Obama credit for it. Trump's temporary gas price obsession was yet another example of his political pandering. Trump picks out an issue with momentary political approval and simply announces that he can solve the problem. That's the demagogic populism of Donald Trump.

Trump's solutions for high gas prices were extremely disturbing: Trump wrote, "if any country in the Middle East won't sell us their oil at a fair market price—oil that we discovered, we pumped, and we made profitable for the countries of the Middle East in the first place—we have every right to take it." Aside from the fact that the United States didn't discover oil in the Middle East and certainly didn't do anything special to make it profitable, that land and that oil doesn't belong to America. And the United States doesn't get to seize the natural resources of other countries on the grounds that their prices are too expensive.

TRUMP THE TAX EVADER

In 2015, Trump told Hugh Hewitt that he "would release tax returns," but now Trump is refusing to follow through. Trump claimed, "I want to release my tax returns, but I can't release it while I'm under an audit." Romney tweeted, "No legit reason @realDonaldTrump can't release returns while being audited, but if scared, release earlier returns no longer under audit." Romney added, "There are more #bombshells or he would release them." As Romney put it, "It is disqualifying for a modern-day presidential nominee to refuse to release tax returns to the voters, especially one who has not been subject to public scrutiny in either military or public service."

Romney knows this topic well, since he faced criticism for delaying the release of his tax returns, including from Trump: "I think Mitt was hurt really very badly by this whole thing with the income tax returns. I believe he should have given them April 1."

In 2011, Trump promised to release his tax returns after Barack Obama released his long-form birth certificate, but Trump never did. In 2014, Trump said, "If I decide to run for office I'll produce my tax returns. Absolutely. I would love to do that."

The reason why Trump is regularly audited has to do with his aggressive tax avoidance and his complex business arrangements. Trump's mentor, Roy Cohn, was infamous for refusing to pay income taxes, and was audited for 20 consecutive years with IRS liens totaling $3.18 million.

Is Trump concealing his tax returns to hide his tax avoidance? The only tax returns from Trump that have been revealed show a man who has paid no income taxes. In 1978 and 1979, Trump claimed a combined income of negative $3.8 million in order to pay no taxes. The only other tax returns from Trump that were revealed came in a case before the New York State Division of Tax Appeals in 1994, where the record included the Schedule C of Trump's 1984 federal income tax return, where he listed no income, yet he deducted $626,264 as expenses. A *New York Times* profile in 1984 called Trump "one of the nation's wealthiest entrepreneurs." Trump complained that he was being taxed twice, but a judge wrote, "The problem at issue is not one of double taxation, but of no taxation."

TRUMP THE COMMON MAN

One of the biggest frauds Trump has perpetrated is pretending to be a defender of the average American. Trump has denounced "the campaign of fear and intimidation being pushed by powerful corporations, media elites, and powerful dynasties. The people who rigged the system for their benefit will do anything and say anything to keep things exactly as they are."

Trump's pseudo-populism is belied by his life as the beneficiary of a powerful real estate dynasty, where he made his money putting his name on the priciest buildings for the wealthiest people. Trump's populist mask is also exposed by his policy proposals that represent the biggest tax cuts for the rich in history. Trump tries to sound like a populist when he declares that "hedge fund guys are getting away with murder" because they pay a 23.8 percent tax rate on "carried interest" rather than the top tax rate of 39.6 percent. But Trump's proposal is to cut taxes on the rich to 25 percent, and to help the hedge fund guys even more: all business income, including that of hedge fund managers, will be taxed at only 15 percent, a cut of more than one-third from the current tax structure that Trump claimed was rigged on their behalf. (Back in 2011, Trump proposed abolishing all corporate income taxes.)

Trump complains that "the financial programs of this country are so tilted in favor of the rich," but his proposals expand that favoritism toward the rich. Trump's claim that his riches would make him a great president must be questioned when much of Trump's success comes from various forms of tax avoidance. The federal budget can't be balanced on a scam. Indeed, it's people like Trump who bear some of the blame for the size of the national debt. Tax avoidance, mostly by the wealthy, results in a huge loss in federal revenues.

Trump has never even said that because he understands all the ways to evade taxes, he would be the perfect person to enact reforms in order to stop all of the tax avoidance by rich people like him. In fact, every proposal Trump has made as a presidential candidate involves massive tax cuts for him and his rich buddies.

TRUMP'S GUT

While Trump's candidacy is based on the idea that he is a brilliant businessman who can easily translate his skills to the government, there is little evidence of Trump's skills. Trump famously says that he thinks with his gut. Trump wrote, "if you are good and you are smart, you can go with your gut." And Trump explained one example of his brilliant gut. He was thinking of buying a property, but his gut held him back. Then "the property was severely damaged by a huge storm." Trump concluded, "my gut instincts had spared me from making a costly mistake. Always listen to your instincts." Trump apparently thinks that his instincts can predict the weather.

Trump declared: "I thought owning the Plaza would be extremely cool, which is sort of my investment policy in life and it seems to work." Trump admitted at the time that economics couldn't justify what he paid for the Plaza, and it was a disaster. Trump's reliance on instinct has often proved to be his undoing. As biographer Timothy O'Brien noted, "he's been a horrible dealmaker. His career is littered with bad deals."

THE ART OF THE DEAL

For Trump, the "art of the deal" is the foundational myth of his business success. Trump says he can make a deal with anyone, and he always makes the best deal. When Trump announced his presidential run, he declared: "We need a leader that wrote 'The Art of the Deal.'" Tony Schwartz, listed as the co-author of the book, tweeted: "I wrote The Art of the Deal. Donald Trump read it." According to Schwartz, "I put lipstick on a pig." Schwartz called Trump a "sociopath" and declared, "I genuinely believe that if Trump wins and gets the nuclear codes there is an excellent possibility it will lead to the end of civilization."

Ironically, Trump made a terrible deal for *The Art of the Deal*. Schwartz's $250,000 advance and half of the royalties made him one of the highest-paid ghostwriters for a single book in the history of publishing. Yet Trump claimed, "He didn't write the book. I wrote the book." Obviously, this is untrue because if Trump had actually written his book, he would be suing his ghostwriter rather than handing over half of his profits. Schwartz reported that Trump read over the manuscript, deleted a few criticisms of influential people he didn't want to offend, and otherwise left it almost unchanged. Howard Kaminsky, the former head of Random House, said: "Trump didn't write a postcard for us!"

For a dealmaker like Trump, ambiguity is the essence of deal-making. Standing on principles is, to Trump, a position of weakness in any negotiation. Predictability means that you can be exploited. In a negotiation between a sane man and a lunatic, the crazy man always wins. To Trump, the extraordinary power of the presidency, to use nuclear weapons or to crash the world economy, would only enhance his negotiating position. While most people are unwilling to think the unthinkable, Trump believes that only a credible threat to destroy the world can maximize your gains in any negotiation. Trump's success (when it has happened) has largely depended upon his willingness to reject bad deals, and to hold his business partners hostage to a threatened bankruptcy.

What Trump fails to understand is that a country is not like a person, or even an individual company. The threat by the American government to go bankrupt would not reduce debt to pennies on the dollar; it would cause a crash in the world economy, lead to global recession, and create greater debt.

THE TRUMP BRAND

Trump has declared, "I've made some of the best branding deals around, especially recently. If our government were as wise with our nation's cash, we wouldn't be in the big mess we are in today." Trump has the same economic qualifications to be president as Kim Kardashian. He is a celebrity who turns his name into massive revenues from reality television and marketing deals.

Everything Trump did to get rich—using bankruptcy law, profiting from government subsidies, and making branding deals—cannot be used by a president to fix the American economy. As bad as Trump's record is, his business experience is even worse: he has never learned from his mistakes because he has always been able to weasel out of them. Trump still believes in his magical ability to make everything right, to do the best deal, and that kind of hubris is a dangerous kind of arrogance for a president to have.

THE KING OF DEBT

Trump has claimed, "I'm the king of debt. I understand debt probably better than anybody." When it comes to accepting responsibility for his debts, Trump often prefers to run away: "I figured it was the bank's problem, not mine. What the hell did I care? I actually told one bank, 'I told you you shouldn't have loaned me that money.'"

And Trump's understanding of the federal government's debt is disturbing: "I have borrowed, knowing that you can pay back with discounts. And I have done very well. I would borrow, knowing that if the economy crashed, you could make a deal, and if the economy was good, it was good, so, therefore, you can't lose." What Trump is talking about is a partial or complete default, or the bankruptcy of the US government.

In response to the backlash against what Trump said, he immediately denied saying it: "People say I want to default on debt—these people are crazy. First of all you never have to default because you print the money I hate to tell you, so there is never a default." So Trump's actual plan to get discounts on the national debt is to print more money and cause massive inflation, which will reduce the real cost of debt, but at a tremendous economic cost to the entire country. This is a terrible idea.

Then, after stating he might default on the national debt or just print money to cover it, Trump claimed that what he really meant was, "if interest rates go up and bonds go down, you can buy debt—that's what I'm talking about. So here is the story, if we have an opportunity where interest rates go up and you can buy back debt at a discount." Unfortunately, although the government could reduce nominal debt by buying new debt at a higher interest rate, that wouldn't improve interest payments, which is the key problem with having debt. Private companies with a liquid cash flow often buy back debt, but that doesn't work with the national debt. If you're running an enormous deficit, you can't solve your problem by borrowing money to buy back debt, because you have to pay interest on the money you borrow.

Trump's inability to understand basic economic concepts shows how his business experience leads him to embrace terrible ideas. Because Trump maintained his wealth with bankruptcies and the threat of default, he imagines that the same magic trick will work with the US economy. Trump's economic plans are among the most dangerous to the American economy ever proposed by a presidential candidate. According to the Tax Foundation, Trump's plans for massive tax cuts would cause the national debt to grow by more than $1 trillion per year over the next decade, even if the tax cuts spurred some additional economic growth. Because Trump's plans to start trade wars are likely to cause an economic recession, Trump's impact would be catastrophic.

THE SCAM OF TRUMP UNIVERSITY

Trump University was a scam that began as a delusion. The delusion was Trump's belief that he could create an online university for $3 million that would establish his "legacy as an educator." At the launch of Trump University in 2005, Trump announced: "If I had a choice of making lots of money or imparting lots of knowledge, I think I'd be as happy to impart knowledge as to make money." But in less than two years, Trump University ran out of money and Trump quickly transformed it into a get-rich-quick scheme to use the Trump name to separate suckers from their money.

Trump's original idea for Trump University was to develop an online university that would provide a practical education for students. Trump declared, "I love the concept of starting what I think will be a great university." He hired high-profile online educators to develop the model for it: "Terrific people, terrific brains, successful, the best." Trump had allocated $3 million in start-up costs for his university, and it was clear that despite his high-profile brand name, the business was another one of his failures.

Roger Schank, a former Yale University and Northwestern University professor, was hired as Trump University's chief learning officer when it began: "I was set up to believe, and this was true for a while, that this was going to be the avant-garde right way to do teaching." But by late 2006, Schank was told he would be dismissed because the school had used up the $3 million that Trump wanted to invest in the project: "At that point, Mr. Trump decided to stop building the online learn-by-doing courses that I was hired to do and do real estate seminars instead. He didn't need me for that." According to Schank, "I don't know if those seminars were shady or not. I wasn't there and I wasn't consulted." Trump had burned through the $3 million he had committed to the idea with no signs of success, and he wanted to cut his losses. Schank reported being told, "we just don't have any more money, and we need to make money quickly in some other way."

Trump restructured the whole business model for Trump University. Trump University made a licensing deal with a Florida company called Business Strategies Group, which began to conduct seminars city-by-city on real estate investing, using the Trump name.

But Trump realized that the name of "Trump University" (and the credibility of those Ivy League professors he had hired) could still be useful. According to Trump, "students who participated in Trump University were provided a substantive, valuable education based upon a curriculum developed by professors from Northwestern University, Columbia Business School, Stanford University and other respected institutions." That's not true. The original curriculum for Trump University was developed by respected professors from elite institutions. But the overpriced real estate seminars that led to the lawsuits against Trump were not developed by professors at all, but by Business Strategies Group, a company that specialized in motivational speeches. The company was run by Mike and Irene Milin, who were "law-bending carnival barkers" with "a long history of battling fraud charges," according to Yahoo! Finance columnist Rick Newman. Trump carefully reviewed all of the marketing material, but never looked at any of the course content.

At the height of the real estate bubble, Trump University was transformed from a failed online education company to a successful wealth seminar scam. Trump University was no different from any of Trump's other branding enterprises. The formula is simple: stick Trump's name on any enterprise aimed at a wealthy customer, and sucker them into paying far more than would be merited. The problem for Trump was that he called it a university. The customers were promised an opportunity to learn Trump's business techniques, and to get rich like him.

Trump University was a classic bait-and-switch con, attracting students with a free seminar that was a sales pitch for a $995-$1,995 executive seminar, which was a sales pitch for a $34,995 elite mentorship program (they were told that these special one-day prices would go up to $48,490 if they didn't act immediately). Students were promised that they would be personally trained by Trump and have their pictures taken with him. All they got was a photo with a cardboard cutout of Trump.

Trump University is now the subject of two class-action lawsuits, and an action by New York Attorney General Eric Schneiderman, alleging fraud, false advertising, and other violations.

Trump University directly targeted the financially vulnerable. One script would ask of prospective customers, "How many of you lost a lot of your 401(k) investment in the market?" Salespeople were encouraged to ask customers if they had a 401(k) or IRA they could use to pay for the course.

One sales manager for Trump University, Ronald Schnackenberg, recounted how he was reprimanded for failing to pressure a financially struggling couple on disability to take out a home equity loan in order to sign up for a $35,000 real estate class. Schnackenberg declared, "I believe that Trump University was a fraudulent scheme, and that it preyed upon the elderly and uneducated to separate them from their money."

Jason Nicholas, a sales executive at Trump University, said it "did not provide a legitimate real-estate education" and was "just selling false hopes and lies." Nicholas said the Trump University instructors were "unqualified people posing as Donald Trump's 'right-hand men.'"

James Harris, an instructor at Trump University, reported: "I was told to do one thing....to show up to teach, train and motivate people to purchase the Trump University products and services and make sure everybody bought. That is it." The only thing Trump University really taught anyone to do was buy more into the scam of Trump University.

While the instructors were described as "hand-selected" by Trump, he admitted that he did not pick them, and Schnackenberg reported that he never saw Trump at all during seven months working at Trump University. According to Schnackenberg, "Trump University was engaging in misleading, fraudulent, and dishonest conduct."

In 2005, Trump University was notified by the state of New York that it was operating as a university with a license in violation of state law, and promised to leave New York. But it didn't, and continued to be operated as Trump University until 2010 after getting a cease-and-desist letter from the state of New York. After a court ruling declared Trump University was an unlicensed educational institution, it was renamed "Trump Entrepreneur Initiative." Trump made millions of dollars in profits, but never donated the money to charity as he had promised.

THE TRUMP FOUNDATION

After the housing bubble burst, Trump's real estate seminars lost the big crowds of gullible customers, and Trump University was shut down. But the lawsuits began to mount.

In September 2013, a few days after it was revealed that Florida Attorney General Pam Bondi was considering whether to join the lawsuit against Trump University, she requested a donation from Trump to her political organization, And Justice for All. The Trump Foundation illegally gave her organization a $25,000 gift, confusing it with a non-profit group that had the same name.

Ironically, Trump regularly calls Hillary Clinton "corrupt" because the Clinton Foundation took money for charitable causes from foreign billionaires who could have been affected by the decisions Clinton made as Secretary of State. There's no evidence that Clinton ever changed a policy to favor a donor or sought a donation from anyone for an action she took, but that didn't stop Trump from declaring, "Hillary Clinton may be the most corrupt person ever to seek the presidency."

By contrast, Trump actually used his foundation in direct violation of federal law. Most foundation grants require a detailed application process including a federal ID number as proof of non-profit status. The mix-up over the different organizations only happened because this wasn't a typical foundation request: it was most likely a directive that came straight from Donald Trump to flatter a politician by providing a gift to what he mistakenly assumed was her nonprofit group.

The Bondi case could be used to argue that not only are Trump's practices at the very least questionable, but they also reveal an incompetent businessman. Using his foundation to bribe a politician could have endangered the foundation's tax status, and should have drawn the attention of prosecutors to a possible act of bribery. But Trump's "donation" could be seen as an attempt to influence an attorney general who ultimately refused to join the lawsuit against Trump University, and became a future political ally.

Trump has a long history of using his foundation in ways that might well be described as self-serving. In 2012, Trump wanted a football helmet signed by Tim Tebow that was part of a charity auction. Trump made the winning bid of $12,000, but he used his foundation to pay the check. It's definitely not legal for directors of charities to use a foundation to benefit themselves, and it's doubtful that the foundation wanted a football helmet. During the 2016 campaign, Trump regularly handed out checks from his foundation to charities at his rallies. Trump ordered his foundation to give more than $150,000 to the American Conservative Union Foundation, which helped him get prime speaking opportunities at the Conservative Political Action Conference, which aided him in his presidential ambitions.

Trump's campaign released a 93-page list of 4,844 gifts Trump made over the past five years, totaling $102 million. But a Washington *Post* investigation discovered that none of these gifts "was actually a personal gift of Trump's own money." Instead, the gifts came from Trump's foundation (which Trump hasn't donated to since 2009) or from Trump's businesses, such as a free round of golf. One donation to Serena Williams never went to her charity; instead, it consisted of a free ride for her on his plane from a Trump resort event, and a free framed photo of himself.

More than half of the $102 million value came from "conservation easements" that actually profited Trump and his companies with dubious tax breaks. Trump agreed not to build homes in an area he owned near his golf course, and instead turned it into a driving range with a bonus tax break.

Trump regularly has promised that he gives the proceeds of an enterprise to charity: his book *Crippled America*; Trump Vodka; Trump University. Trump may be reluctant to release his tax returns due to his lack of charitable donations. Washington *Post* reporter David Fahrenthold asked more than 200 charities about any donations from Donald Trump since 2008, and discovered only one small gift. It took four months and numerous questions from reporters before Trump fulfilled his promise to give $1 million to veterans' groups.

Trump has openly admitted that he donates to politicians in exchange for political favors: "I give to everybody. When they call, I give. And you know what? When I need something from them, two years later, three years later, I call them. They are there for me." Trump noted: "As a businessman and a very substantial donor to very important people, when you give, they do whatever the hell you want them to do."

In 2010, the Texas Consumer Protection Division sought permission to pursue a $5.4 million lawsuit against Trump University, but Texas Attorney General Greg Abbott's office quashed the request. Texas investigators concluded, "Consumers who pay for the three-day course complain that they are taught little useable content. Our review of the course materials reveals that the course teaches legally and ethically questionable real estate investment strategies...." According to former deputy director John Owens, "The decision not to sue him was political. Had he not been involved in politics to the extent he was at the time, we would have gotten approval. Had he been just some other scam artist, we would have sued him." Abbott later received a $35,000 donation from Trump in his run for governor.

CON MAN TRUMP

Trump declared, "Hillary Clinton has perfected the politics of personal profit and even theft. She gets rich making you poor." Such accusations are absurd: Hillary Clinton has never done anything approaching theft, and while she did get rich giving speeches, none of her talks made anybody poor. By contrast, Trump's attack almost exactly describes his own life, and the thousands of people he scammed making millions from Trump University, encouraging them to max out their credit cards for the false hope of learning his real estate secrets.

For all of Trump's dismissive attacks on "losers" and his belief that winning is everything, Trump's core appeal is to the unemployed, the underpaid, the angry, resentful masses who think the American Dream has disappeared and somebody else is to blame. As the candidate for losers, Trump offers his personal promise that he's a winner and can turn them into winners, too. It's the same kind of marketing Trump used for Trump University, with the same deceit and manipulation. The Trump presidency, like Trump University, is only intended to magnify and enrich Trump himself. In both of these scams, Trump depends upon finding people desperate for an easy solution and dumb enough to imagine that Trump can deliver what he says.

One key to a good con is convincing the sucker that a gold mine awaits them if only they will trust the con man to deliver. Trump promised at a rally, "I'm gonna take care of everybody." He told his followers, "I will give you everything. I will give you what you've been looking for for 50 years. I'm the only one." It's rare to find a politician with the hubris to literally promise "everything" if he's elected.

The promises Trump offers as a politician are the same that he offered through Trump University: he will make you wealthy and successful, and it will be as easy as picking him in the voting booth. Politics is the easiest scam there is. Trump University required persuading its students to max out their credit card limits and spend vast amounts of money. But an election requires no investment of time and money from Trump's fans. There are no lawyers waiting to sue for the undelivered promises. The presidency seems to be Trump's ultimate scheme to get fame and fortune at the expense of anyone gullible enough to believe what he says.

3 TYRANT TRUMP

Trump wrote in the opening line of a chapter in his 2011 book, "Your civil liberties mean nothing if you're dead." The problem with this attitude is that it is often truncated to, your civil liberties mean nothing. And based on his history and campaign promises, that's how Trump views civil liberties.

Trump's son Eric Trump once said about his father, "there is no one who cares about our civil liberties more than he does. This is a guy who jumps up and down every time somebody says, 'holiday tree.' No, it's not a holiday tree guys, it's a Christmas tree.'" Trying to stop people from saying "holiday trees" does not prove you are more concerned about civil liberties than anyone else—it proves that you have no real understanding of what civil liberties are or why they should be protected.

According to Donald Trump, "If I'm president, you're going to see 'Merry Christmas' in department stores, believe me, believe me. You're going to see it." But the government doesn't ban anyone from saying "Merry Christmas" in department stores, and it's a violation of religious liberty for a president to try to force everyone in department stores to say "Merry Christmas."

According to Trump, "There's an assault on anything having to [do] with Christianity. They don't want to use the word 'Christmas' anymore at department stores. There's always lawsuits and unfortunately a lot of those lawsuits are won by the other side." Actually, there are no lawsuits banning department stores from using the word "Christmas."

Trump frequently declares his devotion to religious freedom, which he has called "the No. 1 question." Trump has said, "I believe religious freedom is the most fundamental constitutional right we have and must be protected." But his belief in religious freedom seems to depend on whether he agrees with a speaker's religious views.

Pope Francis criticized Trump by saying, "A person who thinks only about building walls—wherever they may be—and not building bridges, is not Christian." Trump responded, "No leader, especially a religious leader, should have the right to question another man's religion or faith." However, challenging the religious values of others is not just the right, but arguably one of the fundamental duties of a religious leader.

Trump was angered when Ted Cruz's father, Raphael Cruz, told a reporter: "I implore, I exhort every member of the body of Christ to vote according to the word of God and vote for the candidate that stands on the word of God and on the Constitution of the United States of America. And I am convinced that man is my son Ted Cruz." Trump declared, "I think it's a disgrace that he is allowed to do it. I think it's a disgrace that he's allowed to say it." Trump wasn't merely saying that Raphael Cruz's views were disgraceful. He felt that Cruz should not be allowed to express such religious opinions.

Of course, the greatest threat to religious liberty proposed by Trump is his call to ban Muslims from entering the country. Trump declared that his proposed ban on Muslims was based on an online poll of Muslims in the United States conducted by an anti-Muslim group that claimed 51% of those polled "agreed that Muslims in America should have the choice of being governed according to sharia." According to Trump, "Sharia authorizes such atrocities as murder against non-believers who won't convert, beheadings and more unthinkable acts that pose great harm to Americans, especially women." However, that's not how most Muslims interpret sharia, particularly in the guise of a manipulative question about Muslims having the "choice" to follow sharia.

The fact that Trump cited a survey of American Muslims to justify a ban on Muslim immigrants indicates that he intends to suppress the rights of Muslims in the United States. In America, Trump has supported a database to track Muslims and announced, "I want surveillance of certain mosques."

Trump has stood by his blanket assertion that "Islam hates us" to justify his ban on Muslims. When he was attacked for his bigotry by a wide range of critics (including his vice presidential nominee Mike Pence, who called the proposal "offensive and unconstitutional"), Trump decided to shift his plan to target nations with a "history of terrorism" (a standard that would include the United States). But Trump merely claimed "it could be an expansion" of his immigration ban to go beyond Muslims. Trump compared his plan to the internment of Japanese-Americans during World War II: "What I'm doing is no different than FDR." And he's right. Trump's proposal is not much different from one of the most shameful violations of civil liberties in American history. Trump admitted that he was willing to violate constitutional rights: "Our Constitution is great. But it doesn't necessarily give us the right to commit suicide."

THE AUTHORITARIAN TRUMP

Trump displays an extraordinary indifference toward human rights. In 1990, Trump talked about the Tiananmen Square massacre in an interview with *Playboy*: "When the students poured into Tiananmen Square, the Chinese government almost blew it. Then they were vicious, they were horrible, but they put it down with strength. That shows you the power of strength." During a 2015 Republican debate, Trump called the Tiananmen Square protests a "riot" that was "kept down" by a "strong, powerful" response from the Chinese government. A leading Tiananmen dissident, Wu'er Kaixi, wrote that Trump is "an enemy of the values that America deeply defines itself by—the same values that have long provided hope to the victims of oppressive power worldwide."

If Donald Trump thinks repression of the rights of your own people is a sign of strength for a powerful government, he may be tempted to engage in that repression against protesters. And that's exactly how he has already approached some of the protests at his own rallies during the campaign, endorsing violence against his critics. At one rally, Trump said about a protester: "I'd like to punch him in the face." At another rally, Trump announced, "If you see somebody getting ready to throw a tomato, knock the crap out of them, would you? Seriously. OK? Just knock the hell—I promise you, I will pay the legal fees."

At one rally, a black protester was sucker-punched in the face by a Trump supporter, John McGraw, who declared, "The next time we see him, we may have to kill him." When asked about the assault, Trump responded by calling McGraw "a very passionate person" and said he "obviously loves his country," and Trump instructed his staff to look into paying McGraw's legal bills. Trump even told the security guards at one of his rallies to steal the coats of protesters and "Throw them out into the cold."

Back in 1990, Trump complained that Russian leader Mikhail Gorbachev was not authoritarian enough: "Russia is out of control and the leadership knows it. That's my problem with Gorbachev. Not a firm enough hand."

That's not a problem for Russia's current leader. Trump and Vladimir Putin have a mutual admiration that's quite alarming, because Trump seems willing to overlook Putin's dangerous authoritarian tendencies: "I've always felt, you know, fine about Putin. I think that he is a strong leader, he's a powerful leader, he's represented his country."

When MSNBC host (and former Republican Congressman) Joe Scarborough told Trump, "Well, he's also a person that kills journalists and political opponents and invades countries. Obviously, that would be a concern, would it not?" Trump replied, "He's running his country and at least he's a leader, you know, unlike what we have in this country." "But again," said Scarborough, "he kills journalists that don't agree with him." Trump replied, "Well, I think our country does plenty of killing also, Joe." Does Trump actually think the United States is killing journalists who criticize the government? Or does Trump just wish that would happen? (In fairness to Trump, he has said about reporters, "I'd never kill them," which would be reassuring, except that the press hadn't realized Trump considered murdering journalists an option he needed to rule out publicly.) Trump refused to criticize Turkey or any other country for human rights violations: "When it comes to civil liberties, our country has a lot of problems, and I think it's very hard for us to get involved in other countries when we don't know what we are doing and we can't see straight in our own country."

Trump has also called for the US government to suppress extremist ideas on the Internet: "We're losing a lot of people because of the Internet. And we have to do something. We have to go see Bill Gates and a lot of different people that really understand what's happening. We have to talk to them, maybe in certain areas, closing that Internet up in some way. Somebody will say, 'oh, freedom of speech, freedom of speech.' These are foolish people. We have a lot of foolish people. We have a lot of foolish people." Closing up parts of the Internet would be an action matched only by authoritarian regimes such as China, and it would be an extraordinary violation of the First Amendment.

Republican Senator Mike Lee from Utah explained why he was refusing to endorse Trump: "I'd like some assurances that he's going to be a vigorous defender for the U.S. Constitution. That he's not going to be an autocrat, that he's not going to be an authoritarian, that he's not somebody who's going to abuse a document to which I've sworn an oath to uphold and protect and defend."

Trump's authoritarian tendencies are a serious concern because no one knows how he might act as president. Even among CEOs, Trump is unusual because he is accustomed to answering to no one but himself. The fact that Trump celebrates the repressive regimes of the world indicates a dangerous tendency to attack civil liberties.

TRUMP AND THE CENTRAL PARK FIVE

Trump has little interest in due process, even when people are innocent of the crimes they're accused of committing. In 1989, Trump spent $85,000 purchasing full-page ads in New York City newspapers saying "these muggers and murderers...should be forced to suffer," advocating the death penalty in New York City for assault, and adding, "Criminals must be told that their CIVIL LIBERTIES END WHEN AN ATTACK ON OUR SAFETY BEGINS!" You don't need to be a card-carrying member of the ACLU to worry about Trump's argument that the death penalty should apply even when no one is murdered, or that civil liberties should end in the name of safety.

Trump's ad was a reaction to a brutal rape and assault of a Central Park jogger, which led to the conviction of five teenagers who were later exonerated. Trump later called the settlement with the falsely-imprisoned individuals a "disgrace," claiming that "Settling doesn't mean innocence" even though DNA evidence identified the actual lone assailant, who confessed to committing the crime by himself. But Trump still believed the detectives who had screwed up the case and allowed the true criminal to escape: "Speak to the detectives on the case and try listening to the facts. These young men do not exactly have the pasts of angels." In Trump's mind, it's perfectly acceptable to falsely imprison young black men for more than a decade based on a crime they did not commit, all because someone tells him they're not angels.

Trump has promised to abuse the president's power to issue executive orders. Trump declared, "One of the first things I'd do in terms of executive order, if I win, will be to sign a strong, strong statement that would go out to the country, out to the world, anybody killing a police man, a police woman, a police officer, anybody killing a police officer, the death penalty is going to happen." According to Trump, "We just can't afford any more to be so politically correct." Trump is apparently unaware that a president cannot impose the death penalty by executive order, especially when dealing with state crimes. But the concept of due process does not interest Trump.

Trump has also announced that as president he would expand the use of executive orders to impose his will on the country: "I'm going to use them much better." Conservative Robert Kagan noted, "In the past, Americans did not know as they voted that their presidents would seek to abuse their executive powers. This time, and indeed for the first time ever, they do." According to Kagan, "Never before has a presidential candidate given more reason to fear that he will run roughshod over democratic institutions and abuse the vast powers of the presidency for personal ends."

TRUMP THE TORTURER

Trump has repeatedly declared his support for torture: "We should go for waterboarding and we should go tougher than waterboarding." Indeed, Trump called for torturing people to death. And he went even further than that, declaring: "The other thing is with the terrorists, you have to take out their families." Upon being told that laws and treaties ban torture, Trump backed down briefly, but he still declared that "We have to play the game the way they're playing the game" and added, "I'm in total support of waterboarding. It has to be within the law, but I have to expand the law."

Trump has claimed that "torture works," calling those who came up with international laws against torture "eggheads." And unlike some advocates of torture, Trump doesn't even care whether torture is effective: "If it doesn't work, they deserve it anyway." After a terrorist attack in Turkey, Trump proclaimed, "We have to fight so viciously. And violently because we're dealing with violent people viciously."

DEFAMING TRUMP

One of Trump's biggest attacks on civil liberties comes from his regular threats to sue reporters for libel if he doesn't like what they write. If elected president, Trump has promised to use his power to suppress the freedom of the press: "We're going to open up those libel laws so when the *New York Times* writes a hit piece, which is a total disgrace, or when the *Washington Post*, which is there for other reasons, writes a hit piece, we can sue them and win money instead of having no chance of winning because they're totally protected." It's notable that Trump's plan for libel law is not about purposely false stories, but "purposely negative" stories, or what he calls "a hit piece."

Trump has used the threat of libel suits to intimidate reporters for most of his life. Trump told reporter Wayne Barrett in 1978, "I've sued twice for libel. Roy Cohn's been my attorney both times. I've won once and the other case is pending. It's cost me one hundred thousand dollars, but it's worth it. I've broken one writer. You and I've been friends and all, but if your story damages my reputation, I'll sue."

In 1984, Trump sued the *Chicago Tribune* and its architecture critic Paul Gapp for $500 million after Gapp called Trump's plan to build the world's tallest building in Manhattan "one of the silliest things anyone could inflict on New York or any other city."

Pulitzer Prize-winning reporter David Cay Johnston wrote that Trump told him he would sue if he didn't "like what you write" about his connections to the mob. It took more than two decades for the documentary *Trump: What's the Deal?* to be released, because Trump's threat of lawsuits scared away broadcasters.

When business reporter Robert Slater started writing a book in 2004 about Trump's approach to business, he was shocked to immediately receive a cease-and-desist order from the Trump Organization's vice-president and assistant general counsel, threatening to "enjoin you from publishing and disseminating the book." The lawyer, Jason Greenblatt, declared that Trump's business strategies were "unique and proprietary to him." The letter also threatened that a book would be illegal as "an unauthorized exploitation of Mr. Trump's name and/or image for purposes of advertisement and/or trade...."

As Slater noted, "I had written numerous books on public figures. Never once had any of them ever hinted that they had a legal basis for preventing me from writing a book about them." Slater wrote that Trump "wanted to control his image fully by controlling as much as he could what was written about him. He was prepared to use whatever resources were available to him, especially the threat of and even the actual use of litigation."

Trump later met with Slater (only because Jack Welch vouched for him) and explained the threat to sue (which he had forgotten about completely): "Well, he doesn't sound so friendly....So I say, 'All right, fuck him. Let's write him a letter and say we're going to sue your ass off if you write false statements.' "

To Trump, libel lawsuits are simply a tool for negotiating better media coverage. Defamation suits are also one of Trump's favorite mechanisms for revenge, since they are the only way he can sue people who haven't signed a contract with him.

Trump argued that reporter Timothy O'Brien committed "actual malice" by citing three unnamed sources who estimated his net worth at only $150 million to $250 million. Trump filed the $5 billion lawsuit in 2009 over O'Brien's book *TrumpNation: The Art of Being the Donald*. Trump offered his perspective on his lawsuit against O'Brien in one of his books. The chapter title was: "When you're attacked, bite back." Trump wrote, "I do not back down. I don't need the money from winning the case—I need to set the record straight and maybe make it harder for other disreputable writers to knock people for the fun or profit of it." He bragged, "his publisher got something they weren't looking for. They obviously didn't know they were dealing with a guy who would eventually write Never Give Up—and actually mean it."

Trump also threatened to sue MSNBC's Lawrence O'Donnell for suggesting he was worth less than $1 billion. In 2006, Trump threatened to sue Rosie O'Donnell, then a co-host on *The View*, after she said he was bankrupt. Trump retaliated in an interview with *The Insider*, labeling O'Donnell "disgusting, both inside and out." He declared, "Rosie will rue the words she said. I'll most likely sue her for making those false statements—and it'll be fun. Rosie's a loser. A real loser. I look forward to taking lots of money from my nice fat little Rosie."

Even parodies of Trump can spark legal threats. In 2013, the satirical newspaper *The Onion* printed a fake opinion piece authored by "Donald Trump" titled, "When You're Feeling Low, Just Remember I'll Be Dead in About 15 or 20 Years." The essay declared, "you can always take solace in the fact that the monstrous, unimaginable piece of shit that is me will stop existing fairly soon." A Trump attorney wrote "the commentary was not written by Donald Trump. The article is an absolutely disgusting piece that lacks any place in journalism even in your Onion. I am hereby demanding that you immediately remove this disgraceful piece from your website and apologize to Mr. Trump. I further ask that you contact me immediately to discuss. This commentary goes way beyond defamation and if it is not removed I will take all actions to ensure that your actions will not go without consequences. Guide yourself accordingly."

When ABC planned a TV movie about the Trump family, Trump announced "I will definitely" sue before he ever saw it. However, he added, "But as long as it's accurate, I won't be suing them." In 2011, after the song "Donald Trump" by rapper Mac Miller turned into a viral YouTube hit, Trump responded by tweeting, "I'm now going to teach you a big boy lesson about lawsuits and finance." Trump threatened to sue *USA Today* in 2012 because Al Neuharth wrote a column calling Trump a "clown."

In 2013, Trump threatened to sue Angelo Carusone, the organizer of a campaign to get Macy's department store to drop Trump as a celebrity spokesperson and remove Trump-branded products from its shelves because of his sexism and his denial of climate change. Trump's counsel accused Carusone of using "mob-like bullying and coercion" and informed him that if he failed to cease and desist, Trump would sue him for no less than $25 million in damages. In 2013, Trump sued Bill Maher for $5 million because he told a joke about offering Trump money if he could prove he wasn't descended from an orangutan.

Trump's presidential run has only increased his propensity to threaten libel suits against any criticism. After the *Daily Beast* published a July 2015 piece reporting that "Ivana Trump once accused the real-estate tycoon of 'rape,' although she later clarified: not in the 'criminal sense,'" Trump lawyer Michael Cohen threatened to sue the publication over the story: "I will make sure that you and I meet one day while we're in the courthouse. And I will take you for every penny you still don't have. And I will come after your *Daily Beast* and everybody else that you possibly know," Cohen said. "So I'm warning you, tread very fucking lightly, because what I'm going to do to you is going to be fucking disgusting. You understand me?" Cohen declared, "You write a story that has Mr. Trump's name in it, with the word 'rape,' and I'm going to mess your life up… for as long as you're on this frickin' planet… you're going to have judgments against you, so much money, you'll never know how to get out from underneath it."

When the *Daily Beast* was doing a story about one of his company's bankruptcies, Trump himself threatened them: "If you write this one, I'm suing you." Trump also indicated that he wanted to sue *Rolling Stone* and the *Huffington Post* to "put them out of business."

When the *New York Times* published a story about Trump's treatment of women, Trump Organization assistant general counsel Jill Martin told CNN that a defamation lawsuit was "a distinct possibility," but eventually the idea was dropped. Trump tweeted during the campaign, "Watch Kasich squirm—if he is not truthful in his negative ads I will sue him just for fun!" For Trump, libel suits are both a tool to suppress criticism and a means of exacting revenge on his enemies who lack his deep pockets to pay for lawyers. As Evan Mascagni, policy director at the Public Participation Project, has noted: "Donald Trump has repeatedly attempted to silence his critics over the years through frivolous lawsuits."

Trump's reputation for suing anybody who criticizes him has a powerful intimidating effect. One *Daily Telegraph* story quoted "an accountant, who did not want to be named for fear of being sued by Mr. Trump . . ." When a casino industry analyst publicly stated how unlikely it was for the Taj Mahal to be profitable, Trump threatened "a major lawsuit" and got the analyst fired. Though the analyst was completely right, Trump has the money to pay lawyers for suits designed to silence any critics.

SILENCING THE MEDIA

Defamation lawsuits are not Trump's only tool for suppressing freedom of the press. Trump announced, "Based on the incredibly inaccurate coverage and reporting of the record setting Trump campaign, we are hereby revoking the press credentials of the phony and dishonest *Washington Post*." The Trump campaign has also revoke press credentials from *Politico*, the *Des Moines Register*; the *New York Times*, the *Daily Beast, Fusion*, Univision, and *BuzzFeed*. No politician in American history has banned more individual reporters and media outlets from covering his events.

When *National Review* editor Rich Lowry went to Fox News Channel to talk about Trump and said, "Carly cut his balls off with the precision of a surgeon," Trump angrily tweeted, "Incompetent @RichLowry lost it tonight on @FoxNews. He should not be allowed on TV and the FCC should fine him!" Beyond the hypocrisy of a candidate who, in front of the TV cameras, called China "motherfuckers" and repeatedly referred to Ted Cruz as a "pussy" objecting to someone saying "balls," it's disturbing that Trump thinks that the job of the federal government is to fine people for saying "balls," and it's particularly disturbing that Trump doesn't understand the fact that FCC regulations only apply to broadcast stations, not cable networks. The FCC fine and banishment demanded by Trump would be unconstitutional under the First Amendment.

If he were elected president, Trump announced that he would force high-level federal government employees to sign legally binding nondisclosure agreements so that staffers couldn't write about Trump (or leak information to the press). Trump declared, "When people are chosen by a man to go into government at high levels and then they leave government and they write a book about a man and say a lot of things that were really guarded and personal, I don't like that." Trump's nondisclosure agreement with his former campaign manager, Corey Lewandowski, convinced a publisher to cancel a $1.2 million book deal. Ironically, Trump has touted a dubious book written by a former Secret Service agent at the White House who disliked Hillary Clinton.

Whether it's punishing his enemies with libel lawsuits, banning Muslims, torturing prisoners, imprisoning women who have abortions, or a long list of terrible policy proposals, Trump is a strong opponent of a free society. Trump poses an unprecedented threat to civil liberties because of his past attacks on free speech, his indifference to due process and human rights, and his authoritarian tendencies.

4 PARANOID TRUMP

When Donald Trump began testing the waters for a possible candidacy for the Republican presidential nomination in 2011, he decided to focus on an unusual topic: Barack Obama's birth certificate. Why would Trump abandon any credibility he might have had in pursuit of an insane theory pushed by the far reaches of the far right? Why would Trump embrace a theory invoked by racists who thought Obama was a secret Muslim born in Kenya? Part of the reason was Trump's desire to appeal to conservatives by proving his anti-Obama bonafides. But there's a much simpler explanation for why he latched upon such a crazy idea as the foundation of a presidential campaign: Donald Trump loves conspiracy theories.

In his political style and in his policies, Trump is bringing something new to presidential politics: a conspiratorial approach to looking at the world. Whether political opponents, foreign enemies, basic public policy, or the media reporting on him, Trump sees conspiracies everywhere.

Trump proudly called himself a "birther" and wrote, "I simply said what everyone in America was thinking: 'Where's the birth certificate?'" Trump imagined that "everyone in America" shared his conspiracy theory.

Trump told Bill O'Reilly about Obama's birth certificate, "maybe it says he's a Muslim." Of course, birth certificates don't list the child's religion, probably because a newborn doesn't have a religion. Nor do Hawaiian birth certificates list the religion of the parents. But the idea of Obama as a "secret Muslim" is found in many of Trump's conspiracy theories about him.

Astonishingly, even after Obama put his birth certificate on the internet for anyone to see, Trump still clung to the craziest of conspiracy theories: "I'm not saying Obama wasn't born in the United States. However, multiple questions still surround the hospital records, his grandmother's statement that he was born out of the country, and his family members' statements that they weren't sure which hospital he was born in. As for the birth certificate I got him to produce, some people have questioned whether it's authentic. Maybe it is, maybe it isn't."

Trump loves to defend a conspiracy theory by appealing to "some people" who doubt reality, and pretending that he's merely asking "questions," not taking a stand. In fact, there were no rational questions about Obama's birth. His grandmother never said Obama was born in Kenya (it was a translation mistake that she immediately corrected during an interview). No reasonable person would expect every relative to know exactly what hospital someone was born in.

In 2015, Trump revealed that he's still a birther. When Anderson Cooper asked him if Obama was born in the United

States, Trump replied: "I really don't know. I don't know why he wouldn't release his records; but, honestly, I don't want to get into it." Asked if he believed Obama was born in America, Trump replied: "Well, I don't like talking about it anymore because, honestly, I have my own feelings. I think he should have taken the $5 million. I don't know why he spent $4 million in legal fees to keep his records away. Nobody has seen his records. I don't know." Obama never spent $4 million to keep his college and passport records secret, because there was no legal basis for revealing them.

And inside of Trump's Obama conspiracy theory, he had another conspiracy theory: "Do you know that Hillary Clinton was a birther? She wanted those records and fought like hell. People forgot. Did you know John McCain was a birther?"

None of this was true. Neither Clinton nor McCain were birthers. The idea that Hillary Clinton secretly "fought like hell" for Obama's birth records is completely false and Trump has never had any evidence for it. But the idea that Clinton was leading a conspiracy to uncover the Obama conspiracy appealed to Trump's conspiratorial worldview. Even better, Trump could claim credit for being more effective: "They couldn't get the records. Hillary failed. John McCain failed. Trump was able to get him to give something—I don't know what the hell it was—but it doesn't matter."

Trump remains a birther, years after Obama released his birth certificate, and years after all of the evidence has proved Trump wrong. But the nature of a true conspiracy theorist such as Trump is that no evidence is ever sufficient: more evidence merely reveals how deep the conspiracy is. Since any document can be imagined to be fake, Trump can dismiss an actual birth certificate ("I don't know what the hell it was") as just an extension of the original conspiracy.

Trump proclaimed, "I was very proud that I was able to finally get him to do something that no one else had been able to do." For Trump, spreading an insane, racist conspiracy theory was not a mark of shame but a great accomplishment. Obama didn't release his birth certificate because Trump demanded it; he released it in order to humiliate the idiots like Trump who had spread this false rumor. For any other politician, this would have been a career-ending act of incomprehensible stupidity.

Trump was willing to imagine a conspiracy theory for every stage of Obama's life. Trump explained away Obama's birth announcement in the 1961 *Honolulu Advertiser* by saying, "an ad like that could have been staged. I don't mean staged at the time, I mean it could have been computer-generated five years ago, eight years ago, two years ago." Most birthers were smarter than Trump, and realized that it wasn't possible to fake a birth announcement and then insert it into every archive copy, (print and microfiche) in the world. Instead, they simply claimed that Obama's family bought a fake ad for a birth that happened in Kenya. Although Trump didn't come up with that conspiracy, he did think it was suspicious that Obama had a birth announcement: "There's something fishy about the whole thing."

In 2011, Trump declared at the Conservative Political Action Conference that "Our current president came out of nowhere."

For Trump, this wasn't a metaphorical critique of Obama's inexperience. Instead, it was literally a conspiracy theory asserting a hidden past about Obama, beginning with his birth certificate and extending through law school. Trump declared, "In fact, I'll go a step further: the people that went to school with him, they never saw him, they don't know who he is. It's crazy." It is crazy, because there's nothing remotely true about it. In reality, many classmates can recall Obama, while one of Trump's classmates at Fordham reported, "No one I know of has said 'I remember Donald Trump.'"

Trump has also claimed about Obama that "he was a terrible student when he went to Occidental. . . . how do you get into Harvard if you're not a good student?" There's no evidence that Obama was a "terrible" student at his first college (and Trump certainly knows nothing about it). Obama was good enough to transfer into Columbia University, and then he was admitted to Harvard Law, where he graduated magna cum laude. But Trump was embracing a fringe conspiracy theory that a Saudi billionaire arranged to get Obama into Harvard because Obama was a secret Muslim agent.

Trump appeals to conspiracy-minded voters. Trump supporters in the 2016 primary were substantially more likely than the supporters of other candidates to agree with the statement, "President Obama is hiding important information about his background and early life." This is clearly code language for the birther movement that Trump helped lead. When a man told Trump at a 2015 rally in New Hampshire, "We have a problem in this country. It's called Muslims," and declared that President Obama was a Muslim and "not even an American," Trump did not object.

Instead, Trump has said this about Obama, "we're led by a man that either is not tough, not smart, or he's got something else in mind. And the something else in mind, people can't believe it. People cannot—they cannot believe that President Obama is acting the ways he acts and can't even mention the words 'radical Islamic terrorism.' " Trump added, "There's something going on. It's inconceivable. There's something going on." Trump used similar language before, following the San Bernardino terrorist attack. "There is something going on with him that we don't know about," he told a group of Jewish Republican fundraisers in 2015.

The phrase "there's something going on" is Trump's standard way of talking about conspiracies without explicitly naming them. In this case, Trump was arguing that Obama had secret sympathies with radical Islam that caused him to fail to stop Islamic terrorism: "He doesn't get it or he gets it better than anybody understands—it's one or the other, and either one is unacceptable."

Trump eventually issued a statement to the press claiming that he "was referring to the fact that at times President Obama seems more in support of Muslims than Israel." But every single time, Trump was talking about Muslim threats to America, not Israel, and there is no conflict between supporting Muslims and supporting Israel. Trump was indeed admitting that the "something" he was talking about was Obama supporting Muslims.

Trump also announced his belief in a conspiracy theory that Obama did not write his own autobiography: "They say *Dreams of My Father* [sic] was genius and they give him full credit, and now it's coming out that Bill Ayers wrote it…that's what started him on this road where he became president." Trump may have found this believable because he never wrote any of his own books and always used ghostwriters. His "co-author" Tony Schwartz tweeted, "I wrote *The Art of the Deal*. Donald Trump read it." Obama, not Bill Ayers, wrote *Dreams from My Father*.

Ironically, Trump is far less transparent than the man he called "the least transparent president in the history of this country." While demanding to see Obama's college records, applications, and passport records, Trump has refused to provide any of this information himself. And while Obama released all his tax records, Trump is the first presidential candidate in 40 years to keep his tax returns secret. Trump announced he had people in Hawaii investigating Obama's birth and "They cannot believe what they're finding," but he refused to say what it was, and has never answered further questions about it. Trump still harps on conspiracy theories about Obama long after they have been discredited. In 2014, Trump tweeted, "Attention all hackers: You are hacking everything else so please hack Obama's college records (destroyed?) and check 'place of birth.'"

Either Trump is a conspiracy nut who actually believes the nonsense about Obama's birth certificate, or he's a lying political manipulator who intentionally promoted a false issue in order to get publicity and support. The truth is that both are probably true. Although Trump's conspiracy theories about Obama are crazy, they are remarkably popular within the Republican Party. One recent poll found that 54 percent of Republicans believe that Barack Obama is a "secret Muslim." Trump's conspiratorial ideas are part of the mainstream in his party: 44 percent of Republicans believe that Obama was not born in the United States.

Obama's race, his imagined Muslim religion, and his liberalism all swirl together in one paranoid stream of thought within today's Republican Party. Obama's blackness made him seem strange and alien to the white voters in the Republican Party, and that helped make it possible for them to believe that he was a secret Muslim, and a foreign agent sent in to destroy America with liberal policies.

One reason why Republicans were willing to nominate a conspiracy nut as their presidential candidate is that conspiracy theories have slowly taken over the Republican Party. Trump saw an opportunity to distinguish himself from other Republican candidates by being willing to embrace those conspiracies. But even if Trump is a cynical opportunist, that doesn't explain why he sees conspiracies everywhere around him. Trump's conspiratorial mindset is the foundation of how he thinks.

In 2012, Trump claimed that Obama had a secret plan with Saudi Arabia to lower gas prices before the election. Trump asserted that Obama "made a deal with the Saudis" and added, "I think he asked for that favor." The irony is that Trump in his 2011 book blamed Obama for high gas prices and condemned him for failing to make a deal with Saudi Arabia to lower those prices.

So even when Trump (falsely) imagined that Obama was doing exactly what Trump had proposed, Trump still saw it in conspiratorial terms to cast suspicion on Obama.

Trump has also claimed that New York Attorney General Eric Schneiderman had been ordered by Obama to sue Trump University: "I'm not a very paranoid person . . . . When he meets with the president and then files a suit, like, 24 hours later, I think yes, I think I've been targeted." According to Trump, "Schneiderman met with President Obama in Syracuse on Thursday—and sued me on Saturday! Same as IRS etc." Trump explained the source of the lawsuit, "They obviously did it very quickly." Only a paranoid person imagines that an attorney general puts together a complex lawsuit in 24 hours to obey a president's order to go after him.

THE UNEMPLOYMENT CONSPIRACY

Trump has claimed that Obama is behind another conspiracy, to conceal the true unemployment rate: "5.3 percent unemployment—that is the biggest joke there is in this country…The unemployment rate is probably 20 percent, but I will tell you, you have some great economists that will tell you it's a 30, 32. And the highest I've heard so far is 42 percent." Politifact rated that claim as "Pants on Fire," the highest level of falsity.

But Trump has repeatedly proclaimed there is a conspiracy to conceal the "real" unemployment rate: "Don't believe those phony numbers, when you hear 4.9 and 5 percent unemployment. The number's probably 28, 29, as high as 35. In fact, I even heard recently 42 percent."

Even the U6 number (which includes people who are underemployed) was only 9.9 percent, nowhere near the numbers that Trump has fabricated to attack the Obama conspiracy of "phony numbers." According to Trump, "I saw a chart the other day, our real unemployment—because you have 90 million people that aren't working. Ninety-three million to be exact. If you start adding it up, our real unemployment rate is 42 percent." The 93 million people who aren't working include every retiree in America, the disabled, stay-at-home parents, teenagers, full-time students, and anyone else who chooses not to work. Trump claimed about the unemployed, "They're sitting home, they gave up, and now they're considered employed."

The method for determining the unemployment rate is fundamentally no different today than it's ever been, but Trump must imagine a conspiracy in order to explain his false claim that today's economy is in terrible trouble. The unemployment rate in May 2016, 4.7 percent, is lower than it was at any time between 1971 and 1996, and far lower than it was at any point during the Reagan Administration that Trump applaud. The unemployment rate is far lower than it was when Barack Obama took office.

TRUMP AND THE NATIONAL ENQUIRER

One sign of a conspiracy theorist is that they regard the *National Enquirer* as a solid source of news. Trump is a big fan. Trump regards the *National Enquirer* ("You can't knock the *National Enquirer*. It's brought many, many things to light") as a more accurate news source than the *New York Times* ("totally dishonest") or other mainstream journalists.

Trump is a good friend of *National Enquirer* CEO David Pecker, and has even suggested that Packer would be a "brilliant choice" to run *Time* magazine. The *National Enquirer* was incredibly supportive of Trump's presidential campaign, praising Trump for having "quietly donated a huge chunk of his fortune to charity" (despite the lack of any evidence that Trump has made such donations) and even ran a three-part series written by Trump to promote his candidacy, "The Man Behind the Legend!"

Meanwhile, the *National Enquirer* smeared Trump's rivals, claiming that Jeb Bush was involved with Miami cocaine smugglers and cheated on his wife, and attacking Bush's daughter Noelle as "a former druggie" who was "overweight" and "dowdily dressed." When Trump's campaign tried to accuse Ben Carson of medical malpractice, the *National Enquirer* helpfully ran a story about "Bungling Surgeon Ben Carson."

When Ted Cruz became Trump's chief rival for the Republican nomination, the *National Enquirer* went after him. The *Enquirer* ran stories accusing Cruz of having extramarital affairs with five women and linking Cruz to the D.C. Madam's escort service.

Then the *National Enquirer* ran a photo claiming that Ted Cruz's father, Rafael, was with Lee Harvey Oswald before he assassinated John F. Kennedy. In reality, the man pictured in the photo was hired from an unemployment line by Oswald to hand out pro-Castro leaflets, and almost certainly had nothing to do with JFK's assassination. More importantly, the idea that someone in an old photo sort of looks like Cruz's father (who was anti-Castro) is not evidence of anything, besides racism.

Trump declared: "His father was with Lee Harvey Oswald prior to Oswald's being—you know, shot. I mean, the whole thing is ridiculous. What is this, right prior to his being shot, and nobody even brings it up. They don't even talk about that. That was reported, and nobody talks about it." According to Trump, "I mean, what was he doing—what was he doing with Lee Harvey Oswald shortly before the death? Before the shooting? It's horrible."

Trump justified his conspiratorial attack on Cruz's father because "He said very nasty things about me." Even the morning after Cruz ended his campaign and Trump was finally declared the Republican nominee, Trump was still clinging to the conspiracy theory about Cruz's father. He cited "the fact that pictures were taken of him and Lee Harvey Oswald" and that "they didn't deny that picture." The pictures were not of Cruz, and they definitely had denied the picture, but Trump still clung to an absurd conspiracy theory even when it ceased to have any political utility for him. Later, Trump claimed that the photo on the sidewalk showed Cruz and "crazy Lee Harvey Oswald having breakfast." Even though the photo had been repeatedly denied by the Cruz and exposed as untrue, Trump claimed: "Ted never denied that it was his father… But they never denied. Did anybody ever deny that it was the father? They're not saying, 'Oh, that's not really my father.' It's little hard to do. It looks like him." Then Trump complained that he was being blamed for raising this issue that he kept bringing up: "I had nothing to do with it."

When an anti-Trump PAC put out an ad with a revealing photo of Trump's wife Melania, Trump immediately imagined a conspiracy involving his rival Ted Cruz, "He sent the photo out, he knew about it," Trump declared. "He knew about it 100%" and added, "I would be willing to bet he wrote the phrase." There was not the slightest bit of evidence that Cruz had ordered the photo to be put out (especially because coordinating with a PAC would be illegal), but Trump immediately imagined a conspiracy in incredible detail, and then hit back against Cruz and his wife.

THE CLINTON CONSPIRACIES

Now that Trump is running against Hillary Clinton, he has shifted some of his conspiracy theories toward her. Trump told an off-the-record meeting of evangelical Christian leaders that "we don't know anything about Hillary in terms of religion." According to Trump, "Now, she's been in the public eye for years and years, and yet there's no—there's nothing out there. There's like nothing out there. It's going to be an extension of Obama but it's going to be worse, because with Obama you had your guard up. With Hillary you don't, and it's going to be worse." Trump is recycling some of the same conspiracy theories he told about Obama's religion and applying them to Hillary Clinton, claiming that mysteriously there's "nothing" about her religion available. In reality, Hillary's Methodist faith is better known than Trump's religious beliefs, and one professor wrote an entire book titled "God and Hillary Clinton."

Trump has attacked the Trans-Pacific Partnership as a "horrible deal" and claimed that: "It's a deal that was designed for China to come in, as they always do, through the back door and totally take advantage of everyone." China isn't part of the TPP. Trump claimed that Clinton "even deleted this record of total support from her book," but Politifact rated Trump's lie "Pants on Fire." Trump lacks a basic understanding with respect to any actual problems with trade agreements.

Trump has also claimed that "Hillary Clinton's State Department approved the transfer of 20 percent of America's uranium holdings to Russia, while nine investors in the deal funneled $145 million to the Clinton Foundation." This was a conspiracy claim debunked many times; Hillary Clinton had nothing to do with the decision.

Trump has gone further, saying that: "To cover-up her corrupt dealings, Hillary Clinton illegally stashed her State Department emails on a private server. Her server was easily hacked by foreign governments—perhaps even by her financial backers in Communist China—putting all of America in danger." Trump's speech included a footnote to a Politico article supposedly proving this, except that the article noted that there was no evidence that Clinton's server had been hacked; by contrast, the State Department's server has been "repeatedly breached."

According to Trump, "Our adversaries almost certainly have a blackmail file on Hillary Clinton, and this fact alone disqualifies her from service." Trump imagines that a Chinese government conspiracy would blackmail her over mysterious personal revelations in her emails. When asked about his evidence for this alleged hacking that disqualifies Clinton, Trump has responded, "I think I read that" and "I heard it," promising "I will report back to you," before concluding, "I don't know if certainty. I—probably she was hacked."

When Bill Clinton had a brief social meeting with Attorney General Loretta Lynch while they were at a Phoenix airport, it was widely condemned as inappropriate even though they both said Hillary Clinton's emails were never discussed. But Trump saw a preplanned conspiracy controlled by Hillary Clinton: "Does anybody really believe that meeting was just a coincidence?" Trump claimed, "Bill's meeting was probably initiated and demanded by Hillary!"

Trump concluded, "Crooked Hillary Clinton knew that her husband wanted to meet with the U.S.A.G. to work out a deal. The system is totally rigged & corrupt!" Such a conspiracy theory makes no sense: The FBI was never going to recommend a criminal indictment on flimsy evidence, and Lynch would never need direct orders from Bill Clinton to support her friends. But Trump saw a conspiracy between the FBI, Obama, and Clinton: "It was no accident that charges were not recommended against Hillary the exact same day as President Obama campaigns with her for the first time."

No issue is too small to be viewed as a conspiracy by Trump. Trump tweeted, "As usual, Hillary & the Dems are trying to rig the debates so 2 are up against major NFL games. Same as last time w/ Bernie. Unacceptable!" In reality, the debates are scheduled by a non-partisan organization more than a year in advance, and two of the 2012 debates were also up against NFL games. The debates avoid low-rated Friday and Saturday nights, and NFL games are played on three out of the five remaining nights. Only a conspiracy nut would think that Hillary Clinton secretly controls the debate schedule to cause fewer people to watch.

But Trump claims to see Hillary as part of a vast conspiracy, the powerless servant of the secret rulers of the world: "Big business, elite media and major donors are lining up behind the campaign of my opponent because they know she will keep our rigged system in place. They are throwing money at her because they have total control over everything she does. She is their puppet, and they pull the strings."

Trump's favorite approach is to recycle old conspiracy theories about the Clintons. Trump declared that Vince Foster, a friend and close advisor to the Clintons during Bill Clinton's presidency, "had intimate knowledge of what was going on. He knew everything that was going on, and then all of a sudden he committed suicide." Trump added, "I will say there are people who continue to bring it up because they think it was absolutely a murder."

Claiming that "people" believe in a conspiracy gives Trump deniability while allowing him to express his actual belief that "it was absolutely a murder." Among the conspiracy nuts, there is little doubt that Hillary Clinton was part of a plot to murder Foster, and Trump clearly shares that viewpoint. Foster's suicide has been investigated many times, including by Independent Counsel Kenneth Starr. There is absolutely no doubt that Foster committed suicide. Even Rush Limbaugh expressed surprise (and approval) for how far Trump has been willing to take conspiracy theories: "Trump has gone to all of this Clinton conspiracy stuff. . . . Nobody else has wanted to touch this stuff ever, any of it."

ROY COHN'S CONSPIRACIES

Trump's love of conspiracy theories can be traced back to Roy Cohn, his lawyer and mentor in New York. Cohn was the infamous assistant to Senator Joe McCarthy during the Cold War who saw Communist conspiracies everywhere, and Cohn was the man who helped teach Trump conspiratorial thinking, to believe that people were out to get him and that he needed to fight back. Cohn also saw conspiracies among those who hated him for his role in McCarthyism. In 1969, Cohn wrote about his enemies, believing that he was being persecuted by indictments for avoiding income taxes and bilking wealthy clients: "I realized that those who did not like what I was doing would be after me for a long time."

In 1973, Cohn first met Trump to help him with the Justice Department's allegations of racial discrimination. Cohn's approach was to sue the government for $100 million for plotting to attack the Trumps and for conspiring to manipulate witnesses and evidence.

When three of his casino executives died in a helicopter crash, Trump privately wondered if it was sabotage, even though the circumstances made that clearly impossible: "Boy, wouldn't the competition love to hurt me in this way." The idea that Trump's casino competitors would love to hurt him by murdering three of his top executives is insane. But Trump loves to imagine a conspiracy against him.

THE JEFF BEZOS CONSPIRACY

When the *Washington Post* announced plans to write a book about Trump (funded with a $500,000 advance from the publisher

Scribner), Trump immediately saw a conspiracy hatched by Jeff Bezos, the founder of Amazon and owner of the newspaper: "We're getting calls from reporters from the *Washington Post* asking ridiculous questions. And I will tell you, this is owned as a toy by Jeff Bezos . . . Amazon is getting away with murder, tax-wise. He's using the *Washington Post* for power so that the politicians in Washington don't tax Amazon like they should be taxed." But the avoidance of state taxes by internet companies has nothing to do with Amazon's influence, and now Amazon pays sales taxes in most states. It might even gain a competitive advantage from fair taxation policies.

Trump has also said this about Bezos, "he thinks I would go after him for antitrust because he's got a huge antitrust problem. Amazon is controlling so much of what they're doing . . . What he's got is a monopoly and he wants to make sure I don't get in."

One analysis of Trump's record on antitrust (including a $750,000 settlement with the Federal Trade Commission for buying gaming stocks in violation of notification rules, an antitrust lawsuit against the NFL, and fighting an antitrust suit for trying to monopolize the Atlantic City casino industry) concluded that it was "difficult to imagine" a Trump administration taking strong action on antitrust allegations. So Bezos would have no reason to order the *Washington Post* to smear a Republican candidate who had never made antitrust enforcement an issue at all.

Trump imagines not only a conspiracy of the *Washington Post* controlled by Bezos, but he even makes up the evidence to support his delusional thinking: "I think he said to somebody. It was in some article, where he thinks I would go after him for anti-trust because he's got a huge anti-trust problem because he's controlling so much. Amazon is controlling so much of what they're doing. And what they've done is he bought this paper for practically nothing, and he's using that as a tool of political power against me and against other people." There was never any article where Bezos expressed fear about anti-trust enforcement by Trump.

Conspiracy thinking has serious consequences. Trump declared, "We can't let him get away with it," and announced that he would retaliate against Bezos if he was elected: "He wants political influence so Amazon will benefit from it. That's not right. And believe me, if I become president, oh do they have problems. They're going to have such problems." Trump is openly announcing that he will use the federal government's law enforcement wing to get revenge upon his political enemies.

Trump's planned abuse of power is all based upon a conspiratorial delusion. There is no indication that Bezos ever told anybody at his newspaper to go after Trump. Marty Baron, the executive editor of the *Washington Post*, denied that the paper's decision to extensively cover a presidential candidate had anything to do with the owner: "I can say categorically that I have received no instructions from Jeff Bezos regarding our coverage of the presidential campaign—or, for that matter, any other subject."

Trump's campaign of vengeance against Bezos is a stark threat to freedom of the press. Trump is saying that if any media outlet writes something critical about him, he will use the government to threaten the press and any other company controlled by a media outlet's owner. This is a shocking message of government censorship, with Trump threatening the economic viability of any media owners who merely allow good journalists to do their jobs and report on Trump.

TRUMP AND THE GLOBAL WARMING CONSPIRACY

Conspiracy theories can have dire consequences when people in power believe them. On one of the most important issues for the world, global warming, Trump is a conspiracy nut who repeatedly dismisses all the scientific evidence as "a total hoax," "mythical," "nonexistent," "pseudoscience," "con job," "canard," and "bullshit."

In 2012, Trump tweeted, "The concept of global warming was created by and for the Chinese in order to make US manufacturing non-competitive." But in a 2016 interview, Trump claimed that his previous assertion of a Chinese conspiracy was a joke: "I know much about climate change. I'd be—received environmental awards. And I often joke that this is done for the benefit of China. Obviously, I joke. But this is done for the benefit of China..." How does one interpret a humorless man who wrote something with utter seriousness, who claims he was joking and then immediately repeats the very same assertion that he just said was a joke?

Among the relatively small group of public climate change deniers, only a few radical extremists believe that climate change is all a hoax, as Trump does. Almost none of them makes the obviously false claim that the climate is getting colder, as Trump does. And even among the tiny number of conspiracy theorists who do think climate change is all a hoax, Trump appears to be unique in blaming the Chinese for it.

The most likely explanation is that Trump's political handlers have recognized that his views on climate change are so crazy and so stupid that they told him to walk back his Chinese conspiracy theories by calling them a joke, but Trump couldn't stop himself from repeating what he truly believed.

Rush Limbaugh praised Trump's attacks on global warming as a conspiracy even if he couldn't bring himself to agree with Trump's theory that China was behind it: "They're mocking Trump 'cause Trump thinks that global warming is a hoax sponsored by the ChiComs to impede our economic growth. It is a hoax. It is a leftist hoax and it may indeed involve the ChiComs, but Trump's instincts on this are correct."

Trump completely denies the scientific facts, says the Earth is getting colder, and blames a conspiratorial "hoax" for all of the overwhelming evidence that proves climate change is happening.

According to Trump, global warming is a conspiracy of scientists plotting together to get rich: "It's a hoax. I mean, it's a money-making industry, okay? It's a hoax, a lot of it." Trump even claimed there were "scientists practically calling it a hoax."

Trump often reports on the weather as if a cold spell in one small area disproves the global fact of climate change: "Ice storm rolls from Texas to Tennessee—I'm in Los Angeles and it's freezing. Global warming is a total, and very expensive, hoax!" He also wrote, "Snowing in Texas and Louisiana, record setting freezing temperatures throughout the country and beyond. Global warming is an expensive hoax!" In 2013, Trump claimed: "Looks like the U.S. will be having the coldest March since 1996—global warming anyone????????" And: "What the hell is going on with GLOBAL WARMING. The planet is freezing, the ice is building and the G.W. scientists are stuck—a total con job."

It takes a conspiracy theory to allow people like Trump to ignore the most basic scientific evidence—global average temperatures. According to NASA, "The 10 warmest years in the 134-year record all have occurred since 2000, with the exception of 1998. The year 2015 ranks as the warmest on record." But a conspiracy theorist can ignore all this evidence because it is corrupted by the conspiracy. Scientific evidence becomes "faulty science and manipulated data" that only proves how powerful the global conspiracy is.

Trump also believes in a conspiracy of scientists to deprive him of one of his most crucial products: hairspray. According to Trump, "You're not allowed to use hairspray anymore because it affects the ozone layer." Actually, the ban on chlorofluorocarbons as a propellant because it damages the ozone layer doesn't affect the hairspray, but Trump doesn't believe in science: "if I take hairspray and I spray it in my apartment, which is all sealed, you're telling me that affects the ozone layer?...I say no way folks. No way. No way." Science says otherwise. If Trump actually lived in a sealed apartment where no air gets in or out, he would suffer brain damage from oxygen deprivation before dying.

THE AUTISM CONSPIRACY

Trump distrusts science because the idea of scrutinizing evidence in a rational way is alien to a conspiratorial mindset. Trump often argues that scientists are part of a conspiracy: "I believe that the movement against asbestos was led by the mob, because it was often mob-related companies that would do the asbestos removal."

Trump tweeted: "Healthy young child goes to doctor, gets pumped with massive shot of many vaccines, doesn't feel good and changes—AUTISM." Trump claims that doctors and scientists are faking the evidence: "I am being proven right about massive vaccinations—the doctors lied."

The proof, according to Trump, comes from anecdotal evidence: "So many people who have children with autism have thanked me—amazing response. They know far better than fudged up reports!" The cornerstone of a conspiracy theory is the idea that people in power are engaging in deception.

Trump went on to claim, "Just the other day, a 2-year-old child went to have the vaccine, and got a fever, now is autistic. I'm in favor of vaccines, do them over a longer period of time, same amount. And I think you're going to see a big impact on autism."

This is Trump's conspiracy compromise. He accepts without scientific evidence that vaccines cause autism, but because opposing all vaccinations is too extreme politically, Trump simply demands a longer gap in vaccinations. There's no scientific basis for either position, but Trump's conspiratorial mindset demands some kind of solution that he is then the hero for proposing. The scientific evidence is overwhelming: there is no connection between autism and vaccines. But Trump views scientists he disagrees with as just another part of the conspiracy.

TRUMP'S WALL OF CONSPIRACY

Conspiracies drive Trump's thinking about almost everything. Trump's signature issue—to build a wall and make Mexico pay for it—was born out of a ludicrous conspiracy theory. When Trump attacked illegal immigration, he joined many other anti-immigrant politicians. But Trump had an unusual analysis of the problem: "Mexico isn't sending us their best." Virtually everyone involved in the immigration debate, pro and con, understands immigration as a problem of individual Mexicans and others from Latin America crossing the border in search of a better life: jobs, education, safety, etc. Not Trump. His conspiratorial mind saw the secret hand of the Mexican government behind it all. Illegal immigration wasn't the product of millions of individual decisions; it was the government of Mexico "sending" bad people.

Trump wrote in 2011, "Have we suddenly become an annex of Mexico's prison system? If so, Mexico should pay for it. I actually have a theory that Mexico is sending their absolute worst, possibly including prisoners, in order for us to bear the cost, both financial and social." Trump's idea to make Mexico pay for his wall was based upon a conspiracy theory that Mexico was smuggling its prisoners over the border.

Trump's attack on Mexican immigrants as rapists was shocking as much for its stupidity as for its racism. But the assertion that all Mexican immigrants are inherently criminals made sense from Trump's conspiratorial point of view. If the government of Mexico was conspiring to send prisoners to the United States, it would make sense that they sent the "worst" people, the rapists and killers. Put in terms of this conspiracy, the decision to build a wall, and to make Mexico pay for it, makes a certain kind of sense: since the Mexican government is the cause of the problem, why shouldn't it pay for the wall?

But how, exactly, was Mexico bringing its prisoners over the border without anyone noticing? How had they managed to keep prisoners from revealing the secret plan after they were caught in the United States? Trump's theory was too idiotic even for conspiracy nuts on the internet to embrace. Only

Trump thinks immigration is a problem caused by a secret Mexican government conspiracy. Trump's inability to comprehend reality means that his policy solutions are doomed to failure.

THE CONSPIRATORIAL THINKER

Trump is deeply influenced by the leading conspiracy theorists in America, and closely follows their work. Trump sat for a half-hour interview on *The Alex Jones Show*. On the show he called Jones's reputation "amazing" and promised that Jones will be very happy with his presidency. In a press release, Trump called it a "great honor" to be endorsed by Carl Gallups, a conspiracy radio show host who spoke at Trump's rally and believes that the Sandy Hook elementary school massacre was a staged "hoax."

To prove his claims about Muslims cheering in New Jersey after 9/11, Trump linked to an article at the Infowars website, run by conspiracist Alex Jones, who is a Truther who has argued that the U.S. government was behind the 9/11 attacks. Interestingly, Trump has pledged that if he is elected, "you will find out who really knocked down the World Trade Center."

Trump even hinted that Supreme Court Justice Antonin Scalia was murdered, "they say they found a pillow on his face, which is a pretty unusual place to find a pillow."

A conspiratorial president is a dangerous thing. When the leaders of the nation are conspiracy theorists, such thinking mutates into a much more dangerous form, where political dissent can be equated with treason and other crimes. Conspiratorial thinkers tend to keep information secret (they don't want to tell their enemies that they're on to them). They also tend to take counsel only from those who support their views, because they don't trust anyone who disagrees. A president who believes that foreign countries are always conspiring against America brings a paranoid style to politics that makes it difficult to build alliances.

Perhaps the most conspiratorial president in history was Richard Nixon, with his "Enemies List" and, of course, Watergate, the ultimate misstep of a conspiratorial-minded administration. Nixon was almost certain to win re-election in a landslide, but he created a paranoid atmosphere in the White House where it seemed reasonable to break into the Democratic headquarters in order to discover the secret plans of Nixon's enemies. And perhaps Nixon saw something of himself in Trump, since he wrote to him in 1987: "Whenever you decide to run for office, you will be a winner!" But if Nixon's paranoia was the worst of any president to date, Trump outdoes him. Trump is paranoid because he thinks everyone is out to get him. But Trump is a conspiracy nut because he sees plots everywhere, even when they don't involve him.

The best way to describe Donald Trump is that he's a Bircher. The John Birch Society was founded in 1958 on a doctrine that was isolationist, anti-Communist, and conspiratorial.

Donald Trump sees the world in terms of secret interconnected plans, and this makes him extraordinarily gullible. Theories that strike most people as implausible and even crazy are treated by Trump as entirely believable. On the rare occasions when interviewers confront Trump about the evidence for his claims, he will often say that he read it on the Internet ("Check out the Internet. Many people say it's not real"), the *National Enquirer*, or cite a long-discredited book. Trump gives a key piece of advice in one of his books: "Be paranoid." Trump also says, "Even your friends are out to get you!"

Trump appears to be incapable of judging evidence, evaluating sources, or distinguishing between fact and fiction. He sees enemies everywhere around him, and secret plots hatched against him at every turn. Trump is unpredictable, irrational, and prone to making mistakes of monumental proportions while dismissing his critics as part of a conspiracy against him.

5 RACIST TRUMP

onald Trump is a racist. He is someone who deeply believes people behave one way or another because of their skin pigmentation. He has made racist statements throughout his life, he has espoused racist policies, and he has embraced support from racists.

On June 16, 2015, after descending an escalator at the Trump Tower in New York City, Trump launched his presidential campaign with a call to deport over 11 million Mexican immigrants in the US: "When Mexico sends its people, they're not sending their best. They're not sending you. They're sending people that have lots of problems, and they're bringing those problems with us. They're bringing drugs. They're bringing crime. They're rapists. And some, I assume, are good people."

Questioned about his unsupported theories, Trump responded, "Well, somebody's doing the raping.... Who's doing the raping? Who's doing the raping?" Trump had no facts to back up any of his bizarre accusations, but Trump is brilliant at seizing political opportunities that other people have ignored.

Such was the case with the immigration issue in the 2016 campaign. Mainstream Republicans were taking moderate positions on illegal immigration, both to appease business owners who need immigrant labor and to try to bring enough of the growing Latino demographic to the Republican Party before it became a permanent minority party for white people. Trump said Republicans are on a "suicide mission" if they give citizenship to the 11 million illegal immigrants in the country, because "every one of those 11 million will vote Democratic."

Trump attacks Mexicans not because he worries about any threat they pose, but because a certain racist base in the Republican Party feels threatened by them and sees Mexican immigrants as the scapegoat for their own economic difficulties. Trump, despite claiming his devotion to the Constitution, announced that he wanted to change the Constitution and eliminate the guarantee of birthright citizenship.

Trump seems incapable of thinking beyond racist attacks and condescending stereotypes like this tweet: "Happy #CincoDeMayo! The best taco bowls are made in Trump Tower Grill. I love Hispanics!" The taco bowl is an American food invented at a Disneyland restaurant, and it's not clear what Trump thinks it has to do with loving Hispanics. As Jeb Bush noted about Trump's tweet, "It's like eating a watermelon, and saying 'I love African-Americans.'"

Back in 1999, Trump was denouncing anti-immigrant isolationists like Pat Buchanan, calling him "a very dangerous man" because "he attacks gays, immigrants, welfare recipients, even Zulus." Trump wrote in his 2000 book *The America We Deserve*, "Pat Buchanan has been guilty of many egregious examples of intolerance. He has systematically bashed Blacks, Mexicans, and Gays." Trump said about Buchanan, "He wants to divide Americans" and called him a "hypocrite." By 2016, Trump was tweeting about Buchanan (whom he once called a "Neo-Nazi"), "way to go Pat, way ahead of your time!" Trump has learned to embrace his own inner Neo-Nazi and attack the Mexicans, too.

THE "MEXICAN" JUDGE

Trump complained that in the lawsuit over Trump University, "I have a judge who is a hater of Donald Trump, a hater. He's a hater." Trump said that Judge Gonzalo Curiel, who was born in Indiana, is "we believe, Mexican" and had "an absolute conflict" in the case. Trump has complained at various times that Curiel was "Spanish" or "Hispanic" and explained, "He's a Mexican. We're building a wall between here and Mexico." When asked if he would object to having a Muslim judge, Trump responded, "That would be possible, absolutely" and said it was "common sense." Under attack, Trump issued a statement that "It is unfortunate that my comments have been misconstrued as a categorical attack against people of Mexican heritage." It's hard to know why Trump thought his categorical attack against people of Mexican heritage was misconstrued.

Republican House Speaker Paul Ryan called Trump's statement "the textbook definition of a racist comment." Senate Majority Leader Mitch McConnell declared, "I object to a whole series of things that he's said—vehemently object to them. I think all of that needs to stop. Both the shots at people he defeated in the primary and these attacks on various ethnic groups in the country."

There has never been a party's presidential nominee who has been so harshly and widely condemned by the Congressional leaders of that party and denounced as a racist. That reflects their fear that Trump's bigoted brand is also tarnishing the name of the Republican Party.

A clearly irritated Trump told his supporters to attack journalists who ask questions about the lawsuit and his comments about the judge. Trump declared, "The people asking the questions—those are the racists. I would go at 'em." In Trump's upside-down world, anyone who criticizes his openly racist comments is the real racist.

THE MUSLIM INVADERS

Mexicans were not the only target of Trump's white nationalist appeals. On Dec. 7, 2015, the 74th anniversary of the attack on Pearl

Harbor, Trump stood up and read his own press release to a crowd: "Donald J. Trump is calling for a total and complete shutdown of Muslims entering the United States until our country's representatives can figure out what is going on." It was a shocking proposal: a total ban on members of a particular religion entering the country. It would also be a clear violation of the First Amendment's protections of freedom of religion.

Under attack for this bigoted stand, Trump quickly began shifting his position in numerous ways. He indicated that leaders of Muslim nations and US citizens who are Muslim would be allowed to enter the country. Then he announced that his entire proposal was "just a suggestion," perhaps unaware that all proposals by presidential candidates are just a suggestion until they're elected and are able to enact them.

Then Trump declared, "I will suspend immigration from areas of the world when there is a proven history of terrorism against the United States, Europe or our allies, until we understand how to end these threats." It wasn't clear if this was an expansion of his proposal to include non-Muslims, or an attempt to limit it.

When Omar Mateen, an American citizen born (like Trump) in New York City murdered 49 people at a gay nightclub in Orlando, Trump falsely claimed that Mateen was "Afghan" and went on to blame immigration for the American-born murderer: "The only reason the killer was in America was because we allowed his family to come here." Of course, that's true of every American-born killer (among which Christians vastly outnumber Muslims) who is not a pure-bred Native American.

Trump collectively blamed all Muslims for terrorist attacks: "The Muslims have to work with us. They know what's going on." According to Trump, "It's like they're protecting each other, but they're really doing very bad damage. And they have to open up to society, they have to report the bad ones." The fact that a Muslim acquaintance of Mateen reported him to the FBI did nothing to change Trump's viewpoint. Trump said there's "very little assimilation" and some Muslim communities "want to go by their own sets of laws." Meanwhile, Trump relied on the old racist canard ("some of my best friends are ___") to justify his stand: "I have many Muslim friends, and they're thanking me...." Trump did not identify who his "many" Muslim friends were.

An audience member at an event told Trump, "We have a problem in this country. It's called Muslims. You know our current president is one. You know he's not even an American," Trump's response was, "We need this question." Then Trump was told, "we have training camps growing where they want to kill us. That's my question: When can we get rid of them?" Trump fully supported the questioner: "We're going to be looking at a lot of different things. You know, a lot of people are saying that and a lot of people are saying that bad things are happening."

After being attacked for his response, Trump tweeted: "Am I morally obligated to defend the president every time somebody says something bad or controversial about him? I don't think so!" But Trump didn't merely fail to "defend" the fact that Obama is an American; Trump openly supported the questioner who falsely claimed Obama was a foreign Muslim.

Trump declared, "I hate the concept of profiling, but we have to use common sense." That's Trump's way of saying that he loves the concept of racial and religious profiling. Trump warned that immigrants were trying to teach "our children how wonderful ISIS is, and how wonderful Islam is." In Trump's twisted mind, there's no distinction between ISIS and Islam. He thinks an entire religion is linked to terrorism.

THE TRUMP ORGANIZATION'S HOUSING DISCRIMINATION

Trump is a racist in part because of his upbringing. Trump grew up in a racist family real estate company that saw black people as bad for business. As the son of a landlord overseeing segregated housing, Trump was taught to regard African-American tenants as a threat to be avoided. Famed folksinger Woody Guthrie, who moved into Fred Trump's Beach Haven apartment complex in 1950, was shocked by the racism there and by Fred Trump's segregated apartments. As he wrote in a song, "Beach Haven looks like heaven/ Where no black ones come to roam!/ No, no, no! Old Man Trump!/ Old Beach Haven ain't my home!"

As openly segregated housing became illegal, some landlords welcomed diversity. Not Fred and Donald Trump (who had become president of the family business in the early 1970s), who continued discriminating against black people. In Trump's first project helping his father, Cincinnati's Swifton Village Apartments, there were several complaints of race discrimination when the Trumps refused to rent apartments to black people, including one case that went to court in 1969 where the Trumps' general manager called the white woman helping a black couple a "nigger lover." The Trumps eventually settled the case by letting them rent the apartment and paying them $1,000, the maximum award allowed for discrimination.

In October 1973, the Justice Department filed a civil rights case that accused the Trump firm, whose complexes contained 14,000 apartments, of violating the Fair Housing Act of 1968. Trump responded by suing the Justice Department for defamation, seeking $100 million in damages, in a case that was quickly tossed out.

The government charged Trump's company with quoting different rental terms and conditions to blacks and whites and lying to blacks that apartments were not available. Testers of different races asked about available apartments, and received completely different answers. Numerous Trump employees reported the company's practice of secretly marking applications of minorities with "C" for "colored" or "#9" to exclude blacks and Puerto Ricans in order to segregate them into apartment complexes filled with minorities.

A former Trump rental agent, Donald Herman, said he was told that "Trump Management believes that Jewish tenants are the best tenants" and knew about the secret racial coding of applicants. Allan Gross, another Trump rental agent, reported that he knew about a code used "to designate which applicants were black or otherwise 'undesirable.'" A Trump worker, Harry Schefflin, said he was personally ordered to rent only to "Jews and executives" and to discourage blacks from renting.

Other Trump employees reported the tactics used to keep out blacks, such as telling black applicants that the rents were much higher than they actually were. Wayne Barret reported, "Three doormen were told to discourage blacks who came seeking apartments when the manager was out, either by claiming no vacancies or hiking up the rents. A super said he was instructed to send black applicants to the central office but to accept white applications on site." One rental agent reported being told directly by Fred Trump not to rent to blacks who said he wanted to "decrease the number of black tenants" and encourage them to "locate housing elsewhere."

A white tester was told by a building superintendent that "he followed a racially discriminatory rental policy at the direction of his superiors, and that there were only very few 'colored' tenants." The tester recalled that they found "a constant pattern and practice of discrimination" at the Trump buildings. Trump never asserted that these were renegade employees who had discriminated on their own; instead, he claimed that no discrimination ever happened, despite the codes and the testers and the overwhelming evidence of discrimination. One of the Trump properties had zero blacks and another was 1 percent black, while a different Trump property was 40 percent black. Trump himself estimated that only 4.3% of his company's apartments were rented to blacks, when the black population of Brooklyn and Queens was many times higher.

There is no doubt that Donald Trump and his father knowingly engaged in racial discrimination and segregation. That shouldn't surprise anyone, considering the degree of racial segregation in housing in 1973 that continues even today. But Trump refuses to admit anything like this happened.

Trump asserted that his company merely discriminated against poor people, not minorities: "What we didn't do was rent to welfare cases, white or black." But nothing in the Trump family's racial coding or discriminatory rules was connected to welfare. The Trump Organization eventually settled the case, refusing to admit guilt but promising to obey housing laws and advertise in black newspapers. The Justice Department called the decision "one of the most far-reaching ever negotiated." But three years after that, the Justice Department charged Trump Management with continuing to discriminate against blacks.

To be clear, Donald Trump didn't create the racist practices at the Trump buildings. His father did. Additionally, there's no evidence that the racism at Trump buildings was much worse than other places in a deeply segregated country. And it's understandable why Trump doesn't want to admit to his personal involvement in racial discrimination or disparage the memory of his late father by telling the truth.

But facts are facts. The evidence of racial discrimination at the Trump Organization apartments is absolutely overwhelming. Trump lied in an affidavit about it. He lied in his books about it. And Trump has consistently lied about this racism his entire life by refusing to acknowledge reality.

It's inconceivable that Trump's father, who seems to have revealed every detail in teaching him the family business, would have skipped over the racist practices that he deemed essential for rentals. And even if Trump, as president of the company, was somehow unaware of what his father believed, he couldn't have missed the obvious evidence from the complaint where multiple rental agents reported a racial code and racist practices ordered from Trump's office, in addition to racial testers proving racist rental rules, and the segregated racial composition of the residents that Trump regularly saw.

Nor did the settlement end racism by the Trump Organization. In 1978, the Department of Justice charged that "racially discriminatory conduct by Trump agents has occurred with such frequency that it has created a substantial impediment to the full enjoyment of equal opportunity."

Trump learned from his early experience that charges of racial discrimination were just a cost of doing business. He responded to legal requirements for equality by public denials, legal threats, obstructionism, and insincere settlements designed to evade the problem rather than ending the racist practices of his company.

TRUMP AND
THE LAZY BLACKS

John O'Donnell, who ran one of Trump's Atlantic City casinos before quitting in disgust, wrote a book about his experiences with Trump. O'Donnell described a dinner conversation with Trump in which they discussed Trump Plaza's financial executive, who was black. When Trump learned that O'Donnell didn't think much of a particular employee, he opened up. Trump said he didn't like him, either, and added: "And isn't it funny. I've got black accountants at Trump Castle and Trump Plaza. Black guys counting my money! I hate it. The only kind of people I want counting my money are short guys that wear yarmulkes every day. Those are the kind of people I want counting my money. Nobody else." Perhaps that comment could be dismissed as a crude racial joke. But not what Trump said next.

Trump told O'Donnell: "I think that the guy is lazy. And it's probably not his fault because laziness is a trait in blacks. It really is, I believe that. It's not anything they can control." When O'Donnell said it wasn't about skin color, Trump disagreed, declaring: "it's a trait." Trump admitted to him, "If anybody ever heard me say that . . . holy shit . . . I'd be in a lot of trouble. But I have to tell you, that's the way I feel."

It seems entirely plausible that Trump, speaking privately with a top executive whom he had learned didn't like a particular employee, would then talk honestly about that employee. In a later interview with *Playboy* magazine, Trump called O'Donnell a "fucking loser" but admitted: "The stuff O'Donnell wrote about me is probably true."

Trump's comment about the black accountant was not merely a racial epithet directed at one employee who dissatisfied him. Instead, Trump was describing a complete theory of racial inferiority about all black people: "it's a trait."

Trump's racism went beyond blacks. O'Donnell also recounted how Trump exploded in anger about the appearance of his chauffeur: "The motherfucker had gray shoes! He looked like some goddamn Puerto Rican. He looked like somebody we picked up from Spanish Harlem."

For most of his life, Trump has often expressed racist ideas about blacks. In 1989, Trump declared: "A well-educated black has a tremendous advantage over a well-educated white in terms of the job market. I think sometimes a black may think they don't have an advantage or this and that…I've said on one occasion, even about myself, if I were starting off today, I would love to be a well-educated black, because I believe they do have an actual advantage."

But this advantage definitely doesn't exist at Trump's companies. In 1992, Trump's casino had to pay a $200,000 penalty for removing black dealers from tables at the request of high rollers. At a 1993 "Calendar Girl" competition, Trump reportedly directed "any black female contestant to be excluded." In 2005, Trump proposed creating a season of "The Apprentice" that would pit a "team of successful African Americans versus a team of successful whites." He said, "Whether people like that idea or not, it is somewhat reflective of our very vicious world."

Trump assures everyone, "I have a great relationship with the blacks. I've always had a great relationship with the blacks." The first sign that you don't have a great relationship with the blacks is when you refer to them as "the blacks." Or when Trump said to a man in the crowd at one of his rallies "Look at my African-American over here, look at him. Are you the greatest? You know what I'm talking about?"

But Trump has directed much of his racism at Barack Obama, from questioning his birth certificate to blaming him for racism. Trump declared, "Sadly, because President Obama has done such a poor job as president, you won't see another black president for generations!" In reality, Obama is far more popular than Trump (and almost every other politician). But it reflects Trump's racist viewpoint when he imagines that no one will vote for a black president again because they don't like Obama. Obviously, that logic never applies to white presidents, no matter how hated they are. Oddly, Trump wasn't responding to any poll indicating that Americans will reject future black presidents; instead, this seems to be an idea that comes from Trump's own racist mentality.

Trump often seems to think that Obama was the leader of black people and responsible for their actions. After violent protests over the murder by police of Freddie Gray in Baltimore, Trump stated: "Our great African American president hasn't exactly had a positive impact on the thugs who are so happily and openly destroying Baltimore!" Trump also suggested that it was racist for black voters to support Barack Obama: "NBC Wall St Journal Poll of African American voters: 94% @BarackObama, 0% @MittRomney. Even worse than Hillary's old numbers. Is that racism?"

On November 22, 2015, Trump retweeted a neo-Nazi chart citing the nonexistent "Crime Statistics Bureau" to show crime along racial lines. According to Trump's chart, 81% of white victims were murdered by blacks. In reality, FBI statistics show that 82% of whites are murdered by other whites. The fact that Trump promoted fake racist crime data without checking it shows how gullible he is. And the fact that Trump could believe that black people commit the overwhelming majority of murders in America shows how racist he is.

TRUMP'S RACIST BUTLER

One of Trump's employees who has been close to him for decades is Anthony Senecal, who worked for Trump at the Mar-a-Lago resort. Trump promoted him to butler, and after Trump split with Ivana, he felt that he no longer needed four butlers, and so he kept Senecal and fired the rest. The *New York Times* reported in March 2016, "Mr. Senecal tried to retire in 2009, but Mr. Trump decided he was irreplaceable," and "he has been kept around as a kind of unofficial historian at Mar-a-Lago," giving tours. Senecal even met Chris Christie along with Trump during a 2016 visit to the property. The article noted, "Few people here can anticipate Mr. Trump's demands and desires better than Mr. Senecal."

Senecal reported that he and Trump originally bonded over their similar political views. But Senecal's views about Barack Obama, expressed on his Facebook page, have drawn a lot of attention: "this prick needs to be hung for treason!!!"

Senecal wrote that it was time for a "SECOND AMERICAN REVOLUTION !!!!!" He wrote: "The only way we will change this crooked government is to douche it !!!!! This might be the time with this kenyan fraud in power !!!!! ... [W]ith the last breath I draw I will help rid this America of the scum infested in its government—and if that means dragging that ball less dick head from the white mosque and hanging his scrawny ass from the portico—count me in !!!!!"

Senecal repeated some of Trump's birther attacks on Obama: "I don't believe he's an American citizen. I think he's a fraudulent piece of crap that was brought in by the Democrats."

Senecal claimed that Obama "is leading the Muslim Brotherhood" and liked to invoke a particular slur for Muslims: "Our current 'president' is a rotten filthy muzzie !!!!!" Senecal wrote about Obama, "look at the number of goat screwing muzzies he is degrading our government with !!!!!" While Trump called for a ban on Muslim immigrants, Senecal ranted: "muzzie shits ... are invading our country." He added, "there are to [sic] many fkn muzzies in America !!!!!"

Senecal told CNN that he wanted to see Obama killed: "Hanging, shooting—I'd prefer he'd be hung from the portico of the White House, or as I call it, the white mosque." Senecal added, "I think it should have been done by the military in the first term. They still have the chance to do it." He noted, "I think he's a fraud and a traitor and I say that on a regular basis, absolutely." Senecal declared that once Obama leaves office, "only a FEW Negroes and josh earnest will even remember him."

Senecal has criticized Hillary Clinton: "Stop the LYING BITCH OF BENGHAZI, NOW—killery clinton !!!!!! She should be in prison awaiting hanging !!!!!!!!" According to Senecal, "I cannot believe that a common murder is even allowed to run (killery clinton)."

Of course, Senecal is a big fan of Trump: "Now comes Donald J Trump to put an end to the corruption in government !!!!!"

However, Trump's campaign issued a statement condemning Senecal: "Anthony Senecal worked within the large staff at Mar-a-Lago from March 5, 1994 through May 15, 2009 until he was terminated. He has not been employed by Mar-a-Lago since then—approximately seven years ago. His statements regarding President Obama and his family are totally disavowed by Donald J. Trump and the Trump Organization. They are disgusting. Mr. Senecal is obviously a very troubled man." But it's hard to believe that Trump was so close to his butler and never had a clue about his racist views.

TRUMP'S WHITE SUPREMACISTS

It's remarkable how many white supremacists have stepped forward to support Trump's candidacy. A few days after Trump announced his presidential run, the *Daily Stormer*, America's most popular neo-Nazi news site, endorsed him enthusiastically: "Trump is willing to say what most Americans think: it's time to deport these people." It urged white men to "vote for the first time in our lives for the one man who actually represents our interests."

An Illinois delegate for Trump with the twitter handle @ whitepride told the *Chicago Tribune*, "With all the racism going on today, I'm very proud to be white." Another nominated Trump delegate (due to a "database error," according to Trump's campaign) was William Johnson, the leader of the white nationalist American Freedom Party, who wrote a book suggesting that all nonwhite Americans should be deported. Johnson formed a Super PAC and paid for pro-Trump robocalls in Utah in which he called himself "a white nationalist" and declared, "The white race is being replaced by other peoples in America and in all white countries. Donald Trump stands strong as a nationalist." According to Johnson, Trump "is allowing us to talk about things we've not been able to talk about." Johnson also set up the Trump Harassment Hotline for Trump supporters who suffer political harassment.

White supremacist Jared Taylor, the founder of *American Renaissance*, declared his admiration of Trump's approach: "And when people start thinking in those terms, Well, wait a minute, are Muslims really of any use to the United States? Then the next step, of course, is to say, Well, are there any other groups that are of no use to the United States? . . . When you start thinking in terms of group differences, then the camel's nose is under the tent. That opens the door to all kinds, all kinds of anti-orthodox, subversive thinking. And so Donald Trump has played a huge role in breaking down the gates of orthodoxy and making it possible to raise these questions in a way that they've never been raised, at a level at which they've never been raised ever before."

Taylor promised, "If there actually is a Trump presidency, he will attract, at all sorts of levels in his administration, people who do think the way we do. Even though they're not publicly associated with racial dissidents, or white advocacy. There will be a great number who will infiltrate his administration, his campaign, his advisers in ways that cannot but be extremely useful both to Trump and to us."

In Tennessee, an independent candidate for Congress inspired by Trump put up a billboard declaring, "Make America White Again." A self-proclaimed "white nationalist" paid for robocalls in Wisconsin endorsing Donald Trump as "presidential" and promising that "he will respect all women and will help preserve Western Civilization." The white supremacist Traditionalist Worker Party announced its plans to go to the Republican National Convention in order to "make sure that the Donald Trump supporters are defended from the leftist thugs."

In January, a white nationalist super PAC paid for a pro-Trump robocall to Iowa voters that said, "We don't need Muslims. We need smart, well-educated white people who will assimilate to our culture. Vote Trump." Trump responded, "I would disavow that, but I will tell you people are extremely angry." When Trump's response to someone calling for "white people" and no Muslims is to say that "people are extremely angry," it shows that Trump shares that racist anger.

TRUMP, DAVID DUKE, AND THE KKK

One of Trump's disturbing acts during the 2016 campaign was his initial refusal to criticize former Ku Klux Klan leader David Duke, who praised Trump as a supporter of white people: "Even though Trump is not explicitly talking about European Americans, he's implicitly talking about the importance of European Americans."

Back in 2000, Trump announced that he was leaving the Reform Party and cited Duke by name as one of the reasons why: "The Reform Party now includes a Klansman, Mr. Duke, a neo-Nazi, Mr. Buchanan, and a communist, Ms. Fulani. This is not company I wish to keep." In his book, *The America We Deserve*, Trump gave Duke as an example of why public financing of elections is a bad idea, because we shouldn't have public funds supporting such a loathsome candidate.

But in August 2015, when Duke endorsed Trump, Trump pretended not to know who he was: "Somebody told me yesterday, whoever he is...." Asked by Jake Tapper in February 2016 whether he would disavow Duke and other white supremacist groups that are supporting his campaign, Trump responded, "Just so you understand, I don't know anything about David Duke, OK?" Trump was asked three times on whether he'd distance himself from the Ku Klux Klan: "I don't know anything about what you're even talking about with white supremacy or white supremacists. So I don't know. I don't know—did he endorse me, or what's going on? Because I know nothing about David Duke; I know nothing about white supremacists."

Trump declared, "I have to look at the group. I mean, I don't know what group you're talking about. You wouldn't want me to condemn a group that I know nothing about. I'd have to look. If you would send me a list of the groups, I will do research on them and certainly I would disavow if I thought there was something wrong. You may have groups in there that are totally fine—it would be very unfair. So give me a list of the groups and I'll let you know."

Tapper responded: "OK. I'm just talking about David Duke and the Ku Klux Klan here, but—"

And Trump replied: "Honestly, I don't know David Duke. I don't believe I've ever met him. I'm pretty sure I didn't meet him. And I just don't know anything about him."

Trump later explained, "I'm sitting in a house in Florida, with a bad earpiece that they gave me. And you could hardly hear what he was saying, but what I heard was 'various groups.'"

But Trump's explanation makes no sense because during the interview, he three times mentioned David Duke's name and three times he talked about white supremacists. So Trump definitely knew that he was discussing David Duke and white supremacists when he refused to criticize them.

Marco Rubio noted, "not only is that wrong, it makes him unelectable. How are we going to grow our party with a nominee that refuses to condemn the Ku Klux Klan? Don't tell me he doesn't know what the Ku Klux Klan is. This is serious." Sen. Tim Scott, a South Carolina Republican, attacked Trump's response: "Any candidate who cannot immediately condemn a hate group like the KKK does not represent the Republican Party, and will not unite it. If Donald Trump can't take a stand against the KKK, we cannot trust him to stand up for America against Putin, Iran or ISIS."

THE GOOFY ATTACK ON ELIZABETH WARREN

When Massachusetts senator Elizabeth Warren started criticizing Trump, he had a ready response: "Goofy Elizabeth Warren, Hillary Clinton's flunky, has a career that is totally based on a lie. She is not Native American." Trump added, "I find it offensive that Goofy Elizabeth Warren, sometimes referred to as Pocahontas, pretended to be Native American to get in Harvard." According to Trump, "What she did is very racist."

In reality, it was Trump's accusations that were racist and totally based on a lie. Before being elected to the U.S. Senate, Warren was a highly accomplished legal expert. There is no evidence that she ever received any special preferences for being Native American, and there is no evidence that Warren ever falsely pretended to be Native American.

Warren reported, "As a kid, I never asked my mom for documentation when she talked about our Native American heritage. What kid would? But I knew my father's family didn't like that she was part Cherokee and part Delaware, so my parents had to elope." Warren noted, "Everyone on our mother's side—aunts, uncles, and grandparents—talked openly about their Native American ancestry." There is some evidence that Warren has a distant Native American ancestor, mentioned in a 19th century marriage license application, but it's not definitive. Even if this is just a family legend rather than a proven fact, you can't blame Warren for believing her family's stories. As Warren noted, "I never asked for and never got any benefit because of my heritage." She never checked a box as Native American in any of her admission or job applications, and never brought it up in any job interviews. Yet Trump claimed, without any evidence, "she was able to get into various schools because of the fact she applied as a Native American and was probably able to get other things."

Reagan Administration official Charles Fried, who chaired the Harvard Law committee that evaluated Warren, declared: "I can state categorically that the subject of her Native American ancestry never once was mentioned." Even if the Harvard Law professors had known about her background, it's ridiculous to imagine that a bunch of rich white male professors from elite institutions would give special advantages to a woman from a working-class background because of their desire to appease the nonexistent Native American constituency at Harvard.

Far from receiving preferential treatment, it's quite likely that Warren has faced discrimination throughout her career. In 2011, Warren was the only Harvard law professor who had graduated from a public university law school.

Even if one day it was proven that Warren has no Native American ancestors, and even if one day someone found any evidence that Warren ever received any advantage for any position because of her Native American claims, it would still be completely false for Trump to claim that Warren "has a career that is totally based on a lie." The only benefit Warren ever received from believing in her family's Native American history was contributing some recipes to a 1984 Native American cookbook called *Pow Wow Chow*.

Trump's personal lies about Warren are aimed at communicating a bigger lie: that white men are the true victims of discrimination in America.

Trump was appealing to that racial resentment when he claimed about Warren, "Her whole life was based on a fraud. She got into Harvard and all that because she said she was a minority." Warren never "got into Harvard," she was hired to teach there, and there is no evidence of any affirmative action benefits she ever received. Warren came from an impoverished family in

Oklahoma, and started working at the age of 13 in her aunt's restaurant. She won a scholarship to George Washington University, and then graduated from the University of Houston and Rutgers Law School. Despite only getting jobs at less prestigious public institutions early in her career, Warren eventually emerged as a star in her field.

Trump, on the other hand, is the perfect example of someone who benefits from affirmative action for rich white guys. Trump's entire life (where he exclusively attended private schools) is a case study in preferential treatment and undeserved advantages. Trump got into an elite private school in New York because his father was on the governing board. Then he was sent to a private military school to deal with his behavioral problems.

Trump attended Fordham University close to home because, his sister Maryanne explained, "that's where he got in." After two years at Fordham University, Trump reportedly had "respectable" grades (Trump said, "I was a good student generally speaking," but one report said Trump "by no means thrived academically in his two years on Rose Hill...he merely went through the motions"). Trump wanted to attend the University of Pennsylvania's Wharton School of Business. According to Trump biographer Gwenda Blair, "he was admitted to Penn after an interview with a 'friendly' Wharton admissions officer who was an old classmate of Trump's older brother." Trump said, "I got in quickly and easily." That's why it's good to have friends in high places.

A *New York Times* magazine profile of Trump in 1984 reported that "the commencement program from 1968 does not list him as graduating with honors of any kind," even though "just about every profile ever written about Mr. Trump states that he graduated first in his class at Wharton in 1968." Trump did not correct these errors, and it's hard to imagine how that false information could have come from anyone other than Trump. In reality, Blair noted, "He acknowledged he wasn't much of a student."

So we can summarize the difference between Warren and Trump: Warren overcame an impoverished background to excel academically, earned a scholarship, and worked her way to the top of her profession. Trump had all the advantages of wealth, was a mediocre student, got into a college using the privileges and preferences of money and power, and then spread lies about his academic record to make himself look smart.

"THEY DON'T LOOK LIKE INDIANS"

Trump has long had a hostile relationship with Native Americans. In 1993, Trump testified before a Senate committee to oppose Indian casinos because they offered competition to his failing Atlantic City casinos. Trump declared that an entire federally recognized tribe, the Mashantucket Pequots, was a fraud: "They don't look like Indians to me and they don't look like Indians to Indians." It's not clear what Trump thinks an Indian is supposed to look like, but Trump's expertise on identifying Native Americans is flawed at best. Trump declared that he might "perhaps become an Indian myself" in order to get an economic advantage: "I think I might have more Indian blood than a lot of the so-called Indians that are trying to open up the reservations."

Even in 2011, Trump stood by his anti-Indian comments from 1993: "Many of them aren't Indians." He recalled, "I'm sitting here with a room full of people that look just like you Steve and just like me. And they have less Indian blood maybe than we do, okay? And they are running reservations. And I'm saying to myself they don't look like Indians. And I didn't relent."

In 2000, Trump anonymously ran ads in some local New York newspapers, trying to shut down a competing casino planned by Native Americans. The ad showed a picture of needles and drug paraphernalia and declared: "Are these the new neighbors we want?" It claimed: "Members of the Mohawk Indian Tribe have a long criminal record … and ties to the mob." Trump had to pay a $250,000 fine for his secret lobbying in violation of state law.

Trump told a Congressional committee: "It's obvious that organized crime is rampant on the Indian reservations." Trump himself has had much closer connections to organized crimes than the Indian tribes, but he repeatedly invoked the mob to try to stop competition: "It will be the biggest scandal since Al Capone and it will destroy the gambling industry."

At a Trump rally in 2016, a conservative talk radio host who supports Trump, Howie Carr, decided to mock Warren by "putting his hand over his mouth and making a 'Woo, woo, woo' noise meant to represent Native American 'war cries.'" The same noise is repeated by crowds when Trump attacks Warren. Trump himself declared about Warren: "She is one of the least productive senators in the United States senate—we call her 'Pocahontas' for a reason." This suggestion that Warren should be given a Native American name because she is one of the "least productive" senators might have been an example of accidental racism on Trump's part, but he has delivered many openly racist comments about Native Americans in the past.

THE WHITENESS OF DONALD TRUMP

Trump's core of support comes from white people who are obsessed with their whiteness. One survey found that "white independents and Republicans who think their identity as whites is extremely important are more than 30 points more likely to support Trump than those who think their racial identity is not important."

Whites who perceive themselves as victims are also strong Trump supporters. According to one analysis of the polls "white Americans who perceive a great deal of discrimination against their race are almost 40 points more likely to support Trump than those who don't think whites face any discrimination." Surveys also found that "whites who think it's extremely likely that 'many whites are unable to find a job because employers are hiring minorities instead' are over 50 points more likely to support Trump than those who think it's unlikely that many whites are losing jobs to minorities."

It's notable that unlike past conservative racist populists such as George Wallace or Jesse Helms, Trump's populist racism is not primarily aimed at attacking African Americans. Instead, he goes after Mexicans and Muslims, two of the fastest-growing immigrant demographics who pose a threat to working-class whites. And because job opportunities for blue collar whites have declined, many of them find these racist arguments economically and emotionally appealing. So Trump is emphasizing unemployment as a major part of his campaign.

A poll of Republicans by the RAND Corporation found that 60.1% of them expressed strong agreement that "immigrants threaten American customs and values," and determined that the stronger a person agrees with that statement, the more likely they support Trump. Trump is taking economic resentment at inequality and funneling it into white nationalism. He is appealing to white working-class and middle-class voters who have suffered from the dramatic increases in wealth inequality in the past three decades.

In fact, Trump supporters are so racist that Trump actually lost delegates because many of his voters refused to vote for Trump delegates who had names that sounded foreign or non-white. In one Illinois district, a Trump delegate named Doug Hartmann received 31,937 votes, but the Trump delegate named Raja Sadiq only got 24,103 votes, which allowed a Ted Cruz delegate to win instead. In another Illinois district, 4,000 Trump voters who supported a delegate named Paul Minch refused to vote for another Trump delegate named Nabi Fakroddin, costing Trump another delegate. Another Trump delegate named Taneequa Tolbert received substantially fewer votes than a Trump delegate with a white-sounding name.

David Letterman said of Trump, "It's all fun, it's all a circus, it's all a rodeo, until it starts to smack of racism. And then it's no longer fun." Trump responded, "there is nobody who is less of a racist than Donald Trump."

Trump is the candidate of racial delusions, a white guy who received every privilege imaginable but who is utterly convinced that his own hard work got him everything, and who complains about the unfair advantages he imagines are granted to women and minorities. Jim Hightower once said about George H. W. Bush, "He was born on third base and thinks he hit a triple." Donald Trump was born in the owner's box and claimed he was "the best baseball player in New York."

6 SEXIST TRUMP

If there is one belief system that fundamentally characterizes Donald J. Trump, it is misogyny. Trump's intense hatred of women, and his long history of strange sexual comments, reflect a mind twisted by sexism. Trump routinely talks about women in terms of their appearance. He said about rival presidential candidate Carly Fiorina: "Look at that face! Would anyone vote for that? Can you imagine that, the face of our next president? I mean, she's a woman, and I'm not supposed to say bad things, but really, folks, come on. Are we serious?"

Incredibly, Trump tried to backpedal and pretend that he never said what he actually said: "Probably I did say something like that about Carly—I'm talking about persona, I'm not talking not about looks." Of course, it's completely clear that Trump's use of the word "face" referred to Fiorina's face, not her persona. He wasn't talking about Fiorina being the face of the Republican Party; he was ridiculing the idea that her ugly face could be "the face of our next president." And Trump was perfectly aware what he was doing, because he added, "she's a woman, and I'm not supposed to say bad things."

Trump then whined, "When I get criticized constantly about my hair, nobody does a story about 'Oh, isn't that terrible, they criticized Donald Trump's hair.'" But the difference is that no competing candidate says that Trump's goofy hair is a disqualification for the presidency. For Trump, who judges women based purely on appearance and believes that everyone else does, too, the face of Fiorina is her primary characteristic of any importance.

At the next Republican debate, Trump tried to walk back his derogatory comments by declaring, "she's got a beautiful face and she's a beautiful woman." Nobody believed him because he was obviously lying. But more importantly, this "compliment" only confirmed Trump's sexist worldview. He didn't apologize and say that candidates should be judged based on their merits rather than their looks. Instead, Trump tried to give the highest compliment he could offer a woman—to call her "beautiful"—even when everyone knows he's lying. Trump would rather tell a small lie about a woman in a condescending gesture of kindness than confront his own sexist attitudes.

Trump has an obsession with attacking the looks of women (but not men) who dare to criticize him. Trump once mailed *New York Times* columnist Gail Collins a copy of her column and wrote across her picture, "face of a dog."

Trump also said this: "Arianna Huffington is unattractive both inside and out. I fully understand why her former husband left her for a man—he made a good decision." To Trump, this is the ultimate insult: the idea that a wife is so ugly she turned her husband gay.

Trump answered his critics who complained about his sexist attacks on the appearance of women: "why is it necessary to comment on Arianna Huffington's looks? Because she is a dog who wrongfully comments on me."

Trump would target any woman who criticized him. Trump attacked Selina Scott of ITV after she did a report critical of him, calling her "unattractive." He sent her angry letters for a decade.

He bragged, "Cher said some nasty shit. So I took on Cher. I knocked the shit out of her and she never said a thing about me after that." For Trump, attacking the appearance of women is not just a sexist impulse; it's a tactic he uses to silence any criticism. Although Trump tweeted that "Cher should stop with the bad plastic surgery," Cher has continued to criticize Trump.

Trump tweeted, "While @BetteMidler is an extremely unattractive woman, I refuse to say that because I always insist on being politically correct." Trump went on to call Midler "disgusting," as well as "grotesque" and "ugly." But judging the appearance of women isn't just a tactic of Trump's, it's a basic impulse that he often can't control. "Looking good" is the highest possible accolade for Trump; after the horrific massacre of more than 80 people in Nice, Trump tweeted: "Our country is totally divided and our enemies are watching. We are not looking good, we are not looking smart, we are not looking tough!" On a more banal level, Trump declared that famed actress Kim Novak should "sue her plastic surgeon." After making this comment, Trump noted, "I didn't think I got in trouble." Like a child unconcerned with the morality of his actions, instead solely obsessed with avoiding trouble, Trump doesn't really care about other people, especially women.

Trump always reserved his harshest attacks for Rosie O'Donnell, such as: "Rosie's a loser. A real loser. I look forward to taking lots of money from my nice fat little Rosie," and "I'd like to take some money out of her fat-ass pockets." It's not surprising that Trump hates O'Donnell. But the fact that he obsessively calls O'Donnell "fat" and a "disgusting pig" reflects how he treats women. According to Trump, "Rosie O'Donnell is disgusting—both inside and out. If you take a look at her, she's a slob. How does she even get on television? If I were running *The View*, I'd fire Rosie. I'd look her right in that fat, ugly face of hers and say, 'Rosie, you're fired.'"

Trump has made even more disturbing comments about O'Donnell: "Rosie's a person that's very lucky to have her girlfriend. And she better be careful or I'll send one of my friends over to pick up her girlfriend. Why would she stay with Rosie if she had another choice?" It's difficult to reconcile this openly immoral attitude with Trump's claims to be a Christian or his appeal among fundamentalist Christians.

Trump has further declared, "Rosie is crude, rude, obnoxious and dumb. She's a slob. She talks like a truck driver." Trump's penchant for swearing is acceptable to him even though he's running for president, because it reflects his ability to speak to the common man. But a woman who swears gets condemned by Trump for talking "like a truck driver."

This attitude toward women is also embraced by Trump's top advisors. His campaign manager, Lewandowski, was charged with assault for grabbing a female reporter's arm during a campaign event. But while this attack got plenty of media attention, few reported on what BuzzFeed News noted about Lewandowski: "more than once, he has called female reporters late at night to come on to them, often not sounding entirely sober." Lewandowski also joked about which female reporters he wanted to "debrief." *Politico* reported that Lewandowski once screamed at a female co-worker, calling her a "cunt."

Victoria Zdrok, a former Playboy Playmate and Penthouse Pet, dated Trump a few times, claiming that he lured her on a date by falsely suggesting that his casinos were looking for a model for an ad. According to Zdrok, "I never met a more narcissistic person than Donald. You feel just like a piece of jewelry when you're with him. For him it's all about looks, appearances, and signing autographs." She reported that Trump told her, "Once you made love to me, you'll never be able to make love to anybody else." When Trump learned she was talking to a reporter about him, Trump denied dating her and predictably attacked her appearance: "She looks like a fucking third-rate hooker."

TRUMP AND THE
BEAUTIFUL WOMEN

The flip side of Trump's attack on "unattractive" women is his propensity for publicly approving of the appearance of women he likes. At a meeting with the *Washington Post* editorial board, Trump declared, "This is a very good looking group of people here," and on his way out of the meeting Trump told one (female) editor, "I really hope I answered your question, beautiful." When *People* senior editor Charlotte Triggs arrived to interview Trump at his office in 2016, his first words to her were, "You're so beautiful." While campaigning, Trump said to a female TV reporter, "I mean, we could say politically correct that look doesn't matter, but the look obviously matters. Like you wouldn't have your job if you weren't beautiful."

Even when running for president, and promising to be more presidential than anyone in history, Trump still thinks that it's entirely appropriate to call a female journalist "beautiful" during an interview for no reason at all. The idea of women as sex objects is so deeply ingrained in Trump's psyche that he can't stop himself from saying wildly inappropriate things to women.

On Howard Stern's show, Trump would often rate the looks of women, as when he said Jessica Chastain is "certainly not hot" and declared about Nicollette Sheridan: "A person who is very flat-chested is very hard to be a ten." Trump complained about

Angelina Jolie, "she's been with so many guys she makes me look like a baby . . . And, I just don't even find her attractive."

When Stern asked Trump about Princess Diana, "You could've gotten her, right? You could've nailed her," Trump proudly responded, "I think I could have." Trump said, "She had the height, she had the beauty, she had the skin—the whole thing." According to Trump, "she was crazy, but these are minor details." The idea that Trump would send Princess Diana flowers (while she was still married) and actively pursue her as a sexual conquest, all while believing that she was crazy, reflects how single-minded Trump is about women. For Trump, "the whole thing" about a woman is her appearance and sex appeal, and never her intelligence or abilities. Even when he is using the murder of a woman by an illegal immigrant for political propaganda, he can't resist referring to the victim as "that beautiful woman."

Trump's obsession with women's looks has a disturbing effect on those around him. His wife, Ivana, got plastic surgery after Trump criticized her appearance. Trump also complained that his wife only hires insufficiently attractive servants in their home. "They're not tens, I can tell you that. I've been very domesticated. It's a sad event." When asked by Howard Stern if he would still love Melania even if she were disfigured in an accident, Trump responded, "How do the breasts look?" because, "well, that's important." Upon being told that Melania's breasts were still okay, Trump said he would "stay with her 100 percent."

Trump is more attracted to women if he thinks they're stupid. Trump once said about Marla Maples, his second wife and mother of his fourth child, "Nice tits, no brains." In his latest book, he twice refers to his "beautiful wife" Melania and calls his children "highly intelligent," a term he never uses in describing Melania. Trump even views women in the business world as sex objects: "the early victories by the women on *The Apprentice* were, to a very large extent, dependent on their sex appeal." Trump once had a female contestant come around the board table and twirl around. At one point, he asked the male contestants on *The Apprentice* to rate the looks of the women: "Who's the most beautiful on the women's team?"

The hiring process for women on *The Apprentice* apparently consisted of Trump judging their looks. At one speech, Trump recalled, "A gorgeous woman got up to ask me if she could audition for *The Apprentice*.... The second I laid eyes on her I knew she was hot, hot, hot! I said, 'Come on up here to the podium, Jennifer. You're hired.'" Reality TV analyst Jennifer Pozner noted that "a penchant for provocative attire seemed to be a job requirement for most of the women selected to compete for The Donald's professional attentions." She added, "Boob-power, not brainpower, is the key to women's success on *The Apprentice*." A former producer on *The Apprentice* noted, "He was always very open about describing women by their breast size" and reported that Trump said about a production assistant, "Who's that hot little girl running around?" On *Celebrity Apprentice*, Trump told a former Playboy Playmate who was a contestant, "It must be a pretty picture, you dropping to your knees." Trump also thinks all women view him as a sex object: "All of the women on *The*

Apprentice flirted with me—consciously or unconsciously. That's to be expected."

All of this made Trump the perfect man to own the Miss Universe pageant. After purchasing it in 1997, Trump promised he would make the "bathing suits to be smaller and the heels to be higher." Trump bragged, "Miss Universe has the best-looking girls in the world. They're much better-looking than the Miss America contestants." In 2005, Trump promoted the show by saying, "If you're looking for a rocket scientist, don't tune in tonight, but if you're looking for a really beautiful woman, you should watch." According to Trump, "You don't give a shit if a girl can play a violin like the greatest violinist in the world. You want to know what does she look like."

The Miss USA pageant had a requirement that contestants parade in front of Trump so he could separate those he found sexually appealing from those he did not. One of the contestants, Carrie Prejean, wrote about this in her book, *Still Standing*: "Some of the girls were sobbing backstage after [Trump] left, devastated to have failed even before the competition really began...even those of us who were among the chosen couldn't feel very good about it—it was as though we had been stripped bare."

After Alicia Machado won the Miss Universe title, she gained weight, and Trump threatened to fire her unless she went on an extreme diet. She reported, "I said, 'I don't want to do this, Mr. Trump.' He said, 'I don't care.'" Trump publicly mocked her: "She's eating a lot. You could say she's an eating machine." He wrote about her "sitting there plumply."

The Miss USA organization denied entry to contestants who have ever been married or "given birth to, or parented, a child." Trump's pageant was purely about treating women as sex objects. And the knowledge that a woman has a child, or has given birth before, makes them seem less sexy to Trump.

While Trump was treating women like sex objects in the Miss Universe pageant and on *The Apprentice*, he also applied a double standard, attacking women for being sexual. In 2007, Trump signed a deal with Fox to develop a television show called *Lady or a Tramp*? Trump declared, "We are all sick and tired of the glamorization of these out-of-control young women, so I have taken it upon myself to do something about it. I am creating a real-life version of *My Fair Lady* with my company Trump Productions. This show is all about getting a second chance and transforming for the better; the idea is genius and the show will be huge." *Variety* described it as "a reality-competition series in which girls in love with the party life will be sent to a charm school where they will receive a stern course on debutante manners. Trump will exec produce the show and possibly come on air to evaluate contestants' progress."

Trump promised to be deeply involved in casting his tramps: "the best casting will be by going into the various clubs and picking them out. That's when you really see somebody in terms of what we're doing." Trump said, "Unfortunately, who knows that scene better than I do? Somebody's got to do it." The announcement for the show sought "rude and crude party girls…younger women who are 18-30, love to party and full of attitude." To help women achieve the height of "class," the show also planned to recruit prostitute Ashley Alexander Dupré, famous for her involvement with New York Governor Eliot Spitzer.

By 2009, this ill-conceived and unoriginal rip-off of *Ladette to Lady* and *Charm School* was renamed *The Girls of Hedsor Hall* and shown on MTV, with promoters promising that it "will take a group of American girls out of their wild and crazy lifestyles, fly them to England and enroll them in Hedsor Hall, an English finishing school, to teach them how to become proper women." The summaries of the women in the show reflected Trump's sexism:

Brianna: "is she willing to embrace the steps needed to become a respectable woman?"

Lillian: "is a wild, gutter-mouthed girl who parties five nights a week and doesn't think twice about hitting on another woman's man at a nightclub."

Amanda: "is now attending college, but there's no degree in sight unless she manages to reform her wicked ways." What were those wicked ways? "Strip poker, beer bongs and wet T-shirt contests."

Jen: "thinks she is better than everyone and admits to being 'snobby.'"

Hillary: "This pink haired chick likes to get drunk and doesn't hesitate to show off her bare booty when she drinks.... Hillary is rough around the edges and drinks like she's one of the boys."

Maddy: "Her memory is so ruined that she can't even remember the name of the college she once attended."

As a summary of the show put it, "Jennifer had been told more than once by Mrs. Shrager to remove her make-up, and when Mrs. Shrager noticed that her make-up was on once again during cooking, she crossed the line, and yelled at Jennifer to get out of the kitchen and take off her make-up."

The *Lady or a Tramp?* concept reflected Trump's misogyny and hypocrisy. Women were treated as sex objects and put on TV to show off their bodies. At the same time, they were attacked by Trump as "tramps" for being exactly what he wanted them to be.

TRUMP'S SEXUAL CONQUESTS

While Trump has denounced women as tramps, he has bragged for decades about his numerous sexual encounters. Trump claimed, "*Famous* women—I can't give you their names—but *famous* women have now been calling the newspapers, their agents have been calling, saying they were with me, trying to get their pictures in as one of the so-called conquests." Trump actually believed that famous women were urging newspapers to report that they had sex with Trump, who thinks he is a man so masculine and admired that any *famous* woman would benefit immensely from the public knowing that they had sex with him.

There aren't any independent reports about any women bragging about having sex with Trump, let alone any famous women who intentionally leaked the news to the press—and the media silence about these sexual encounters certainly couldn't have been because they feared a lawsuit from Trump. In fact, the reverse was happening, where Trump was planting false stories in the press about famous women sleeping with him.

There is almost nothing that makes Trump prouder than his ability (frequently mentioned by him) to have sex with famous women. As he bragged: "Oftentimes when I was sleeping with one of the top women in the world I would say to myself, thinking about me as a boy from Queens, 'Can you believe what I am getting?'"

Trump also reminisced about the good old days of Studio 54: "I would watch supermodels getting screwed, well-known super-models getting screwed on a bench in the middle of the room. There were seven of them and each one was getting screwed by a different guy." These bizarre scenes, if they are not the product of Trump's vivid sexual imagination, seem to have reinforced Trump's view of women purely as sex objects. Trump bragged in 2013 about his sex life, "I went through beauties."

Trump made his money the traditional way: he inherited it. But he also made (and lost) money in the male world of high-end real estate and construction. He spent his leisure time using women as ornaments to hang from his arm in a world of celebrity. Asked to describe the "ideal company" for him to spend time with, Trump replied, "A total piece of ass." At a 2007 speech on success that began with cheerleaders greeting his entrance on the stage, Trump declared, "the girls—we're supposed to call them women, but they're girls to me—the girls, you can stay the entire speech." Surrounding himself with models and sex objects, Trump found it easy to see women as "girls" and focus on their sexual desirability.

Bragging about his sexual prowess is just another part of his misogyny. Trump once declared about himself, in the third person, "Love him or hate him, Donald Trump is a man who is certain about what he wants and sets out to get it, no holds barred. Women find his power almost as much of a turn-on as his money."

Trump views women as deceptive and dangerous: "Women have one of the great acts of all time. The smart ones act very feminine and needy, but inside they are real killers." According to Trump, "There's nothing I love more than women, but they're really a lot different than portrayed. They are far worse than men, far more aggressive." And the sexuality of women is what makes them threatening to Trump. He wrote about the great realization he had regarding women: "Their sex drive makes us look like babies." Trump, projecting his own ideas, thinks women are sexually obsessed, and for him that justifies treating them all as sex objects, because that's what they really want. And he blames women for controlling men with their sexuality: "I have seen women manipulate men with just a twitch of their eye—or perhaps another body part."

Bragging about penis size is another common theme for Trump. When Gloria Allred sued him, Trump called TMZ and publicly offered to show her his genitals: "I think Gloria would be very very impressed with my dick." Marco Rubio responded to all of Trump's "little Marco" cracks by saying at a rally, "Have you seen his hands? You know what they say about men with small hands? You can't trust them." At the next debate, Trump responded, "he referred to my hands—'if they're small, something else must be small.' I guarantee you there's no problem. I guarantee." It's not clear why Trump thinks a small penis would be a problem, either for Trump's sexual activity, or more importantly for the job of President of the United States. As CNN.com reported in its headline about the debate: "Donald Trump defends size of his penis." For Trump, this metaphorical act on national television of pulling his dick out and waving it around to impress women is part of how he views masculinity.

Rubio's small hands attack came out of an insult that *Vanity Fair* editor Graydon Carter once launched against Trump in *Spy* magazine, calling him a "short-fingered vulgarian." The "vulgarian" insult apparently didn't bother Trump. But the idea that he has small fingers (and the apparent correlation with the size of his penis) became an obsession of Trump's. Carter reported, "To this day, I receive the occasional envelope from Trump. There is always a photo of him—generally a tear sheet from a magazine. On all of them he has circled his hand in gold Sharpie in a valiant effort to highlight the length of his fingers." What kind of lunatic does that? The answer is, a man deeply worried about his masculinity, who thinks that the size of his penis is a measure of not just his sexual worth, but his manliness as well.

Trump's view of women as sex objects is a deeply disturbing form of sexism that would affect his ability to work with female employees, relate to female leaders around the world, and pursue policies to help women achieve equality. How can Trump fight discrimination against women in the workplace when he believes in hiring woman based on their looks, and when he opposes married women working?

Trump's misogyny, of course, also impacts his view of masculinity. For Trump, virtually every interaction is a symbolic fight to display dominance and control. Macho posturing isn't just an act for Trump; it's the essence of his being.

That's a particularly dangerous trait for an American president. The job of president requires diplomatic skills. If Trump had been president during the Cuban Missile Crisis, it's easy to imagine him launching nuclear weapons and starting a global war because backing down would be a display of weakness. Although the dangers today are less serious than during the Cold War, Trump embraces a threatening kind of machismo.

Trump's approach to foreign policy is a reflection of his distorted masculinity. He wants to be simultaneously isolationist and bellicose. He wants to stay out of any foreign entanglements, but he wants to prove he's a tough guy by viciously attacking anyone who might be a threat. His strongest argument for being an effective president is that other countries will be so terrified of his irrational masculinity, and his unpredictable aggression, that they will be too scared to stand up against the United States.

Trump's life has been shaped by sexism: the sexism of a domineering father he admired and wanted to surpass, the sexism he absorbed from spending his life in the construction industry, and most of all, the sexism of celebrity culture that he watched from afar and then spent his life trying to join. And of course, the sexism of politics.

TRUMP AND INCEST

Trump's view of women as sex objects extends to his daughter Ivanka. Trump said about her, "she's really something, and what a beauty, that one. If I weren't happily married and, ya know, her father...." Trump has often made these kinds of sexual comments: "I've said if Ivanka weren't my daughter, perhaps I'd be dating her." When Donald Trump uses the word dating, he means having sex with his daughter (in one book, Trump bragged about models, "I have been able to date (screw) them all"). Trump even said about Ivanka, "she's got the best body."

Amazingly, Ivanka is not the only daughter Trump has sexualized. *On Lifestyles of the Rich and Famous* in 1994, Trump was asked about one-year-old Tiffany Trump, and what characteristics the baby got from Donald and from Marla. Trump responded, "I think that she's got a lot of Marla. She's a really beautiful baby. She's got Marla's legs." Trump then added, "We don't know whether or not she's got this part yet," cupping his breasts, "but time will tell."

Too many people focus on the disturbing incestuous tone of Trump's comments about his daughters, such as when he says about Ivanka, "she does have a very nice figure" or when Trump listed his daughter after being asked by Howard Stern to name the "three hottest chicks you've seen." They miss the equally disturbing sexist undertone—the idea that women are valued for their looks, and that young women in particular are valued as ornaments to decorate the lives of older men.

TRUMP THE TRADITIONALIST

Even by the standards of Republican politicians, Trump has an extraordinarily backward view of the role of women in society: "For a man to be successful he needs support at home, just like my father had from my mother, not someone who is always griping and bitching." For Trump, a woman's place is in the home, and her role is to support her husband without complaint. One of Trump's favorite movies is *Pulp Fiction*: "My favorite part is when Sam has his gun out in the diner and he tells the guy to tell his girlfriend to shut up: 'Tell that bitch to be cool! Say: "Bitch be cool!"' I love those lines." Trump's philosophy of women is that they should be beautiful and quiet and subservient. Trump views women in very paternalistic terms: "They know I'm going to take care of them, I'm going to protect them."

Trump is strongly opposed to women in the workplace: "I think that putting a wife to work is a very dangerous thing. I don't want to sound too much like a chauvinist, but when I come home and dinner's not ready, I'll go through the roof, okay?" These conservative views of women extend to his skepticism about hiring working mothers: "She's not giving me 100 percent. She's giving me 84 percent, and 16 percent is going towards taking care of children."

Trump does not believe in men taking care of children. Trump declared, "I know friends who leave their business so they can spend more time with their children, and I say, 'Gimme a break!' My children could not love me more if I spent fifteen times more time with them." Trump was asked in 2005 about having a child with his new wife, and he responded, "I like kids. I mean, I won't do anything to take care of them. I'll supply funds and she'll take care of the kids. It's not like I'm gonna be walking the kids down Central Park." Ivana Trump said in one interview about her children, "the first one was a boy, which was fantastic, the pressure was off." It says something important about Trump that his wife felt under pressure to deliver him a son.

Trump even blamed his first divorce on the error of allowing his wife to work: "My big mistake with Ivana was taking her out of the role of wife and allowing her to run one of my casinos in Atlantic City, then the Plaza Hotel. While she did an excellent job at both, I could have hired a manager who also would've done a very good job. The problem was, work was all she wanted to talk about. When I got home at night, rather than talking about the softer subjects of life, she wanted to tell me how well the Plaza was doing, or what a great day the casino had. It was just too much . . . I soon began to realize that I was married to a businessperson rather than a wife. It wasn't her fault, but I really believe it wasn't my fault either. It was just something that happened." While it's unusually considerate for Trump to acknowledge that Ivana's desire to be a businesswoman in addition to a wife was not her fault, for Trump, the purpose of women is to be sex objects, and when they start to focus too much on business, they become less attractive as sex objects.

Trump once expressed "his hope that she'd get bored in Atlantic City and agree to return quietly to her duties as a wife and mother of their three children." When Ivana Trump briefly cried during her goodbye speech at the Trump Castle, Trump went to the microphone and mocked her: "That's why I'm sending her back to New York. I don't need this, some woman crying. I need somebody strong in here to take care of this place."

And Trump also criticized having women in the military, blaming it for sexual assault by soldiers: "26,000 unreported sexual [assaults] in the military—only 238 convictions. What did these geniuses expect when they put men and women together?" To Trump, women don't belong in the workplace, especially a traditionally male area such as the military. He puts the blame for rape not on the rapists (or the commanders who fail to stop it), but on the policy of allowing women equal working opportunities. Trump believes that discriminating against women is a good thing, and part of the natural order.

Trump's recent attention to sexual assault in the military seems aimed at banning women from working opportunities altogether, not due to his opposition to rape. In 1992, Trump defended boxer Mike Tyson, claiming that he was "railroaded" after being convicted of rape: "You have a young woman that was in his hotel room late in the evening at her own will. You have a young woman seen dancing for the beauty contest—dancing with a big smile on her face, looked happy as can be." Trump also suggested Tyson should be allowed to pay "millions and millions" of dollars for rape instead of serving jail time. In 2016, Trump went to Indianapolis, where Tyson was convicted of rape, and praised Tyson's endorsement of him: "Mike Tyson endorsed me. I love it . . . You know, all the tough guys endorse me." When he was asked about Tyson's rape conviction, "I don't know anything about his trial. I really don't."

Trump's view that rich men should be allowed to get away with rape may come from a very personal place. Former *Newsweek* reporter Harry Hurt III described Trump's history of assault in his book, *The Lost Tycoon: The Many Lives of Donald J. Trump.* In 1989, Trump had scalp-reduction surgery for his bald spot. He blamed Ivana for the painful results, because she had suggested the doctor. According to Hurt, Trump held down Ivana's arms, pulled hair from her scalp, and tore off her clothes. Hurt wrote: "Then he jams his penis inside her for the first time in more than sixteen months. Ivana is terrified . . . It is a violent assault. According to versions she repeats to some of her closest confidantes, 'he raped me.'" Trump's lawyers pressured the author to include a "A Note to Readers" from Ivana in the book: "As a woman, I felt violated, as the love and tenderness, which he normally exhibited towards me, was absent. I referred to this as a 'rape,' but I do not want my words to be interpreted in a literal or criminal sense." It is not particularly comforting to know that Trump's lawyers pressured a statement out of his ex-wife that asserted Trump was so brutal and violent that it felt like rape, but did not necessarily meet the legal requirements of rape. Unless Trump revokes the non-disclosure agreement imposed on Ivana, we may never know the truth about the details of what happened.

Incredibly, Michael Cohen, special counsel at The Trump Organization, defended his boss in 2015 by saying, "You're talking about the frontrunner for the GOP, presidential candidate, as well as a private individual who never raped anybody. And, of course, understand that by the very definition, you can't rape your spouse." Cohen even repeated this astonishing claim: "It is true. You cannot rape your spouse. And there's very clear case law." In reality, marital rape has been explicitly banned in every state since 1993, and in New York since 1984. The notion that Trump's lawyer promoted marital rape as legal, decades after it was belatedly banned, is shocking. Cohen admitted, "I made an inarticulate comment—which I do not believe—and which I apologize for entirely."

And Trump's alleged attack on Ivana is not the only rape accusation against him. According to a lawsuit Jill Harth filed, after a business meeting with Trump ended at his estate in Mar-a-Lago, Trump bragged that he would be "the best lover you ever have" and "over the plaintiff's objections forcibly prevented plaintiff from leaving and forcibly removed plaintiff to a bedroom, whereupon defendant (Trump) subjected plaintiff to defendant's unwanted sexual advances, which included touching of plaintiff's private parts in an act constituting attempted 'rape.'" The lawsuit claimed that on January 9, 1993: "Trump forcefully removed (her) from public areas of Mar-A-Lago in Florida and forced (her) into a bedroom belonging to defendant's daughter Ivanka, wherein (Trump) forcibly kissed, fondled, and restrained (her) from leaving, against (her) will and despite her protests." Harth's lawsuit was withdrawn around the same time that Trump reportedly agreed to settle a lawsuit with her husband's company. Trump's attorney, Michael Cohen, claimed: "There is no truth to the story at all. The plaintiff in the matter, Jill Harth, would acknowledge the same." But Harth said she "never" recanted the complaint and tweeted, "Bad enough I had to go through sexual harassment over 20 years ago and now it's all public."

In another lawsuit, Trump was accused of raping a thirteen-year-old girl: "Plaintiff was enticed by promises of money and a modeling career to attend a series of parties, with other similarly situated minor females, held at a New York City residence that was being used by Defendant Jeffrey Epstein. At least four of the parties were attended by Defendant Trump." According to the suit, "Defendant Trump initiated sexual contact with Plaintiff at four different parties. On the fourth and final sexual encounter with Defendant Trump, Defendant Trump tied Plaintiff to a bed, exposed himself to Plaintiff, and then proceeded to forcibly rape Plaintiff. During the course of this savage sexual attack, Plaintiff loudly pleaded with Defendant Trump to stop but with no effect. Defendant Trump responded to Plaintiff's pleas by violently striking Plaintiff in the face with his open hand and screaming that he would do whatever he wanted." Another woman certified in the lawsuit, "I personally witnessed four sexual encounters that the Plaintiff was forced to have with Mr. Trump during this period, including the fourth of these encounters where Mr. Trump forcibly raped her despite her pleas to stop."

Trump's office declared, "There is absolutely no merit to these allegations. Period." And there's no evidence that any of this true—except for the part about Trump's association with Jeffrey Epstein, who spent more than a year in prison for soliciting an underage girl for prostitution. Epstein's little black book included fourteen private telephone numbers for Trump and his family. Trump publicly embraced Epstein before he was criminally charged, telling a journalist: "I've known Jeff for fifteen years. Terrific guy, he's a lot of fun to be with. It is even said that he likes beautiful women as much as I do, and many of them are on the younger side. No doubt about it—Jeffrey enjoys his social life." Considering that Trump routinely dated women much younger than himself, the fact that he referred to Epstein liking women "on the younger side" indicates some awareness of Epstein's pedophilia. Did Trump attend Epstein's sex parties? Did he ever see him with underage girls before he praised the sex offender as a "terrific guy"? Plenty of other rich and famous people (including Bill Clinton) were friends with Epstein. But Trump might be the only one who noted Epstein's love of young women while praising him publicly.

Trump once noted, "I've known Paris Hilton from the time she's twelve, her parents are friends of mine, and the first time I saw her she walked into the room and I said, 'Who the hell is that?' At twelve, I wasn't interested . . . but she was beautiful." Despite Trump's denials, it's clear that he was interested in a twelve-year-old girl because he considered her startlingly beautiful, although he realized that he could not publicly admit to it.

But it's that allegation of sexual assault against Trump by his ex-wife that is the most troubling aspect of Trump's past. Ivana is under a gag order from her divorce settlement that bans her from talking about her marriage to Donald without his permission, and she obviously wants to avoid alienating her children who work for Trump. On July 28, 2015, Ivana released a statement declaring, "the story is totally without merit. Donald and I are the best of friends and together have raised three children that we love and are very proud of. I have nothing but fondness for Donald and wish him the best of luck on his campaign."

Although Ivana has now denied being raped, she has not specifically said that the details in the original story were wrong. Nor has Trump himself ever denied any of these details, or released Ivana from any legal liability without preconditions so that she could speak the truth.

TRUMP'S BLOODY "WHEREVER"

Donald Trump does deserve to be defended against one unfair accusation of sexism, when he made comments about TV host Megyn Kelly and her blood: "She gets out there and she starts asking me all sorts of ridiculous questions, and you could see there was blood coming out of her eyes, blood coming out of her . . . wherever."

Critics attacked Trump, accusing him of referring to menstrual blood. Conservative RedState.com editor Erick Erickson disinvited Trump from his RedState Gathering, stating: "I just don't want someone on stage who gets a hostile question from a lady and his first inclination is to imply it was hormonal. It just was wrong." Competing presidential candidate Carly Fiorina tweeted, "Mr. Trump: There. Is. No. Excuse."

Trump denied this accusation: "Only a deviant would say that what I said was what they were referring to, because nobody can make that statement. You almost have to be sick to sort of put that together, I think." According to Trump, "Who would say that? I went to the Wharton School of Finance, I was an excellent student, I'm a smart person."

Trump explained, "I was going to say nose and/or ears, because that's a very common statement, blood flowing out of somebody's nose." It seems likely that Trump was trying to depict

Kelly as being so angry that her eyes were bloodshot and blood was coming out of her nose. But he probably hesitated when he realized that it was ridiculous to claim that Kelly had blood streaming out of her nose. Perhaps the spectacle of Trump getting into a fight with a woman and her ending up with a bloody nose was not exactly the image he wanted to present. So Trump trailed off from his unplanned meandering thought, as he often does.

The alternate explanation, that Trump was referring to Kelly's menstrual blood, makes little sense. Trump's point was that Kelly was fundamentally biased against him, not that she was irrationally under the influence of her menstrual cycle. So it would be strange for Trump to make a traditional sexist argument dismissing outspoken women as being "on the rag" (although Trump's often incoherent arguments still make it a plausible interpretation).

What really makes it difficult to believe that Trump was referring to menstrual blood is his aversion to women's bodily functions. Trump views women as purely sex objects, so he is far too sexist to think of women as having basic biological functions. Menstrual blood is beyond his comprehension. Here's what he said when Hillary Clinton, like other candidates, took a bathroom break during a debate: "I know where she went—it's disgusting, I don't want to talk about it. No, it's too disgusting. Don't say it, it's disgusting." When a lawyer deposing Trump in 2011 asked for a break to pump breast milk for her infant daughter, Trump started screaming at her, "You're disgusting, you're disgusting." If the thought of women breastfeeding or even using the bathroom is too disgusting for Trump to contemplate, there's no way that he was thinking about menstrual blood in the middle of an interview.

The menstruation interpretation also doesn't fit with the particular way Trump was insulting Kelly. Trump wasn't making the traditional sexist argument that Kelly, as a woman, was acting unstable and emotional due to her period. On the contrary, Trump was complaining that Kelly consistently was biased against him. He wanted to attack Kelly as an unfair and permanent enemy, not blame her period for the harsh questions she asked.

The overwhelming focus on what Trump meant by talking about Kelly's "wherever" distracted everyone from the fact that Trump three times had used a sexist insult against Kelly: "Bimbo."

Trump offered his usual defense for twice promoting offensive tweets that used the "bimbo" term against Kelly: "That's a retweet. That's different." But Trump also personally tweeted this about Kelly: "I refuse to call Megyn Kelly a bimbo, because that would not be politically correct. Instead I will only call her a lightweight reporter!" That's how Trump prefers to say something politically incorrect: by explicitly stating what he would call someone except that it's not politically correct. So it's clear that Trump believes Kelly is a "bimbo," he's just afraid to say it himself.

Trump could have called Kelly "stupid," as he would have if he were attacking a man. But the word "bimbo" allows him to describe Kelly as stupid and simultaneously insult her as someone whose professional success is due purely to her physical appearance. It's a particularly ironic insult for a man like Trump. Trump calls female journalists "bimbos" because that's exactly how he would hire women if he ran a media network. He assumes that the rest of the world must also hire women journalists based solely on their appearance because that's what he would do. Trump's use of the word "bimbo" is not only a crude sexist insult; it's also a reflection of Trump's fundamentally misogynist worldview.

When Kelly informed Trump that he had called her a "bimbo" many times, he smiled slightly and said, "excuse me," suggesting that hateful comments about women were just a joke to him. The media spent far more attention imagining what a "wherever" might have meant than focusing on what Trump's use of "bimbo" definitely meant.

TRUMP AND ABORTION

Trump's inability to understand women contributed to perhaps the worst gaffe of his campaign, when he announced (and then quickly withdrew) a plan to put women who have an abortion in prison. Trump's strange odyssey on abortion reflects his lack of any core values and his indifference to women.

In 1989, Trump co-sponsored (but didn't attend) a dinner organized by the National Abortion Rights Action League (NARAL) to honor its former president. In 1999, when Trump was contemplating a run for president, Tim Russert asked him about abortion, and Trump responded, "I'm very pro-choice. I hate the concept of abortion. I hate it. I hate everything it stands for. I cringe when I listen to people debating the subject. But you still—I just believe in choice."

This was the standard pro-choice position, and a position that was (and is) very popular in the country. Trump, who was plotting a potential run on the Reform Party ticket, was aiming his remarks at a general election.

But as Trump realized that a third party run would not work, and that he needed to seek the nomination of the Republican Party, he also realized that a pro-choice position was deadly to his chances for the Presidency. And so, as he put it, "I have evolved. I talk about evolving all the time." Of course, Trump almost never talks about "evolving" because that requires admitting that he was once wrong. Abortion is the one exception. Trump said, "Planned Parenthood should absolutely be defunded" and supported a government shutdown in order to stop funding of women's health care by Planned Parenthood. Then Trump completely reversed himself, announcing that he "would look at the good aspects of it."

When Trump was questioned by Chris Matthews in 2016 about abortion, he was finally forced to confront in detail a position that he had thought about very little. Asked how a ban on abortion would actually work, Trump said, "Well, you go back to a position like they had where they would perhaps go to illegal places but we have to ban it." That's Trump shrugging off with indifference the plight of women getting back-alley abortions. But since the anti-abortion movement doesn't care about this problem, Trump was still on safe ground.

Trump's real mistake came when Matthews pressed Trump on whether he believes there should be punishment for abortion if it were illegal. "There has to be some form of punishment," Trump said. "For the woman?" Matthews asked. "Yeah," Trump said, nodding.

Trump realized that a pro-choice Republican had no chance of succeeding in a Republican primary, and so his position evolved. But because Trump's new pro-life position had no substance behind it, because it was pure political pandering, Trump had no real understanding of the nuances. Trump knows so little about Roe v. Wade that when was asked about the case and the legal doctrine of the right to privacy that underpins it, Trump responded: "What does that have to do with privacy? How are you equating pro-life with privacy?"

Trump didn't realize that the anti-abortion movement had long ago decided that doctors, not women, should be the ones punished for abortion. In answering Matthews' question, Trump said, "people in certain parts of the Republican Party and conservative Republicans would say yes, they should be punished." So Trump thought he was appeasing the far right.

Punishing doctors effectively prevented abortion from happening, while the threat of punishing women who had an abortion undermined political support for banning abortion. When Trump declared that "there has to be some form of punishment" for women, he was simply reaching a logical conclusion: if abortion is illegal, then women who have abortions are breaking the law, and lawbreakers must be punished. That was, after all, precisely the logic of Trump's opposition to illegal immigrants which had been so popular among the Republican electorate: illegal immigrants are breaking the law, and they need to be punished by deportation. But the racism of Trump's anti-Mexican stand was very different than the sexism of his anti-woman position. With abortion, Trump was talking about criminalizing something that has been legal across the United States for more than 40 years.

That's why Trump's remark was so offensive to the anti-abortion movement: not because they thought he was morally wrong, but because he accidentally exposed a deceptive tactic activists were using against women. Trump removed the pretense that the anti-abortion movement is trying to help protect women.

Trump's simplistic logic, borrowed from his anti-immigrant position, ultimately backfired on him. Trump's campaign quickly issued a statement completely reversing course, while quoting Trump as saying, "My position has not changed."

Trump later explained his abortion answer this way: "As a developer and as a businessman, I'm not sure I was ever even asked the question, are you pro-life, pro-choice?" That's perfectly understandable, although most people have actually thought about the issue of abortion without being asked by a reporter. But what's particularly strange is that a year after beginning a campaign for the Presidency, Trump had put so little thought into where he stands on one of the most important political issues of our times that he could not come up with a coherent response.

Trump's answer on abortion revealed to anti-abortion conservatives that he was both insincere and incompetent. He was the worst of all worlds, a pandering political hack who is too lazy to research what he is supposed to say.

DISPLAYING WOMEN

As Trump put it, "You know, it really doesn't matter what they write [about me] as long as you've got a young and beautiful piece of ass." For Trump, beautiful women are the refutation to anybody who insults his looks or his abilities. If he has a beautiful "piece of ass" at his side, he is immune from critique.

David Brooks argued that under Trump's misogyny, "Women are objects men use to win points in that competition. The purpose of a woman's body is to reflect status on a man. One way to emasculate a rival man is to insult or conquer his woman." When Tucker Carlson once mocked him on air, Trump called the pundit and left a voicemail: "It's true you have better hair than I do. But I get more pussy than you do." Sexual bragging is part of Trump's essence.

In a 2001 interview on Stern's show, he got into a shouting match with gossip columnist A.J. Benza over a woman they both dated. Trump bragged about stealing Benza's girlfriend: "I've been successful with your girlfriend, I'll tell you that. I took her away like he was a dog." Benza reported on Trump's bizarre seduction techniques: "He sends things—paper from the news that he has, all the clippings of all his articles that he sends her. Circles his name and writes 'billionaire.'"

Trump promised Benza, "A.J., any girl you have, I can take from you—if I want. Any girl you have, I can take from you. You're full of shit. So any girl you have, I can take. That I guarantee. And that was proven before." For Trump, sex is just another deal to be done. Women, like buildings, are trophies to show his dominance. When real-estate developer Leonard Stern financed a documentary critical of Trump, Trump responded by spreading a false rumor that Stern's wife repeatedly phoned Trump's office "asking for a date." Trump offered to retract the rumor if Stern killed the documentary.

He told Barbara Walters in 1990, "I think the hunt is always fun, whether it's deals, whether it's women, whether it's anything." To Trump, women are not much different from buildings. Trump wrote: "Beauty and elegance, whether in a woman, a building, or a work of art, is not just superficial or something pretty to see."

Trump once told a writer, "You can go ahead and speak to guys who have four-hundred-pound wives at home who are jealous of me, but the guys who really know me know I'm a great builder." Even when Trump is talking about other men, he rates them based on the appearance of their wives.

One of Trump's worst tactical mistakes came when, angered by an anti-Trump Super PAC that ran a commercial with a racy photograph of his wife from her modeling days, he blamed Ted Cruz, and immediately threatened to "spill the beans" about Heidi Cruz. Apparently the only "beans" Trump had was his belief that Heidi Cruz is ugly. Trump retweeted a photo from one of his supporters that depicted his wife Melania side-by-side with a less attractive photo of Cruz's wife. As Newt Gingrich noted, "Tweeting about, or repeating a tweet about Mrs. Cruz, is just utterly stupid."

But Trump can't help himself. When dealing with an enemy, he has no boundaries. He will cross any line; even an enemy's wife is subject to his wrath. And when he attacks women, he will always return to their appearance.

Trump excused his attack on Heidi Cruz and others by claiming, "I attack men far more than I attack women. And I attack them tougher." That's actually true. But Trump insults men even more frequently than he insults women because Trump is operating in the male-dominated worlds of big business, politics, and news media, so when he inevitably attacks everyone in his path, men are usually the targets.

Los Angeles Times columnist Meghan Daum argued, "Is being a crude, shallow boor when it comes to women tantamount to being a misogynist? Not when you're also a crude, shallow boor when it comes to men as well. Trump's grotesqueness is an equal opportunity deal." But Trump attacks men and women very differently. Men are usually called "liar" or "loser" or "moron" by Trump (one of the rare exceptions, when Trump called Ted Cruz a "pussy," was a sexist insult Trump used to demean his rival by comparing him to a woman).

What makes Trump a misogynist is the way that he insults women, and the way that he compliments them. When Trump insults a man, he almost never describes him as "fat" or "ugly." By contrast, a large proportion of Trump's insults against women involve their appearance. Trump is not a misanthrope, he's a misogynist.

TRUMP AND HILLARY

In *The Art of the Comeback*, Trump included a large photo of himself posing with Hillary Clinton: "The First Lady is a wonderful woman who has handled pressure incredibly well." Trump was a big donor to her campaign, and even invited her to his third wedding. For Trump, Hillary Clinton was just another celebrity to boost his sense of self-importance. In 2008, he even endorsed her: "I know Hillary and I think she'd make a great president or vice-president."

All of that changed when Hillary Clinton became his likely opponent for president. Suddenly, Hillary became the "worst Secretary of State in the history of the United States" when Trump began his campaign in 2015. Trump called her "an embarrassment to our country." Yet Trump never said anything like this when Clinton was actually Secretary of State.

Trump also often talked about Hillary Clinton in sexual terms, as when he said about the 2008 campaign, "She was favored to win, and she got schlonged." And he also retweeted, "If Hillary

Clinton can't satisfy her husband what makes her think she can satisfy America?" For Trump, the chief job of a woman is to sexually satisfy men, and Hillary Clinton's imagined failure to satisfy her husband was evidence that if she was not competent at her primary job, she would not be a good president.

Trump did not hesitate to condemn Hillary for allowing her husband to campaign for her: "Hillary Clinton has announced that she is letting her husband out to campaign but HE's DEMONSTRATED A PENCHANT FOR SEXISM, so inappropriate!" For Trump, who has demonstrated a penchant for sexism his entire life, the double standard is remarkable, especially since Trump called Bill Clinton a "great president" in 2008 when Bill was campaigning for Hillary and had the exact same past. Yet Trump complained about Hillary, "She's got one of the great women-abusers of all time sitting in her house, waiting for her to come home to dinner." And Trump even managed to be sexist while pretending to care about sexism, since he was condemning a woman for the actions of her husband. Trump accused Hillary of being an "enabler" of "one of the great woman abusers of all time." Trump claimed "a major book's been written about it, and it's a book that's a very well-respected book. And it was not a pretty picture, what she did." Trump was referring to *The Clintons' War on Women* that was co-written in 2015 by his longtime close adviser, Roger J. Stone, Jr. Stone founded the organization Citizens United Not Timid (CUNT) to attack Hillary. Stone also accused Hillary of leading a conspiracy to murder John F. Kennedy, Jr. (who died in a plane crash). Stone tweeted that "The MURDER of JFK, Jr.

will be the subject of my next book #Clintons #guilty" and "JFK Jr was planning on running for NY Senate seat @HillaryClinton wanted. Poor bastard." Trump has never distanced himself from the crackpot views of one of his top consultants.

Trump is using traditional sexist insults to attack Clinton. He said about Hillary: "She doesn't have strength or stamina. She's not a strong enough person to be president." The idea that women are too weak (both emotionally and physically) has been the excuse men have used for most of human history to exclude them from public life.

Trump famously depicted his rival Jeb Bush as "low energy." But the fact that Trump insulted a man in similar terms doesn't exempt Trump from the charge of sexism. Trump was trying to feminize Jeb Bush by calling him low energy. And it is notable that Trump typically reserved the words "strength" and "stamina" for Hillary, while calling his male opponents "low energy."

Trump claimed as proof of his stamina assertions about Hillary, "She'll do a couple of minutes in Iowa, meaning a short period of time. And then she goes home." It's crazy to imagine that Hillary Clinton was only spending a few minutes at a time campaigning in Iowa. When Clinton had to leave Iowa, it was to do more fundraising, not because she was too tired.

Although Trump is older than Hillary, and would be the oldest person ever elected in the first term as president, he tries to avoid attention to his advanced age by depicting his opponents as physically weak and too feminine. In Trump's eyes, a great president is all about displaying strength and vigor.

Trump declared about Hillary, "she's playing the woman card really big. I watched her the other day and all she would talk about was, 'Women! Women! I'm a woman!'" For Trump, who regards women as decorations, even a small degree of attention to how policies affect women is tantamount to obsession. Clinton devotes only a small portion of her campaign to talking about the needs of women, but Trump hears nothing but her yelling, "I'm a woman!"

Once a woman was his clear opponent, he announced, "Frankly, if Hillary Clinton were a man, I don't think she'd get 5 percent of the vote." Trump is so oblivious to reality that he thinks women get all the advantages and opportunities in life and men are never given a fair chance in politics or anywhere else, despite the overwhelming evidence to the contrary.

If Donald Trump were a woman, she would not be a billionaire real estate mogul, she would not be a celebrity famous for firing people, she would not be a serious political candidate, she would not get close to 1 percent of the votes Trump has received, and she would never be the Republican nominee for president. Trump's political success is only possible because of the double standards that favor men.

TRUMP, THE MISOGYNIST

Here is what Trump said in 1992 about women, according to a *New York Magazine* article: "You have to treat 'em like shit." Trump denied ever saying that, but he often denies saying things that he is recorded saying, and this comment is perfectly in line with Trump's attitude toward women. When Howard Stern asked Trump if he said that, Stern followed up by asking if he treated women with respect. Trump was unusually honest: "I can't say that either."

Trump has changed his position yet again. Today he says, "Nobody has more respect for women than Donald Trump!" And that's true, in a sense. Nobody respects women for their physical beauty more than Trump. And since Trump thinks that's the only reason to respect women, it means he respects women more than anyone else.

Trump embodies nearly every value and double standard of an extreme misogynist. He makes sexist comments evaluating women based on their appearance. He attacks women he opposes as "fat" and "ugly." He routinely sexualizes women while attacking women for being sexual and denouncing them as "tramps." He brags about his sexual conquests, and treats women as ornamentation. He demands traditional wives, and discriminates against working women. Trump represents the very worst kind of sexist, and he is the most abusive hater of women to ever be a major candidate for president in modern times.

7 CARELESS TRUMP

Donald Trump is the candidate of political incorrectness, which as many have noted, is an excuse to belt out any sort of bigotry and intolerance. Trump has declared: "I think the big problem this country has is being politically correct. I've been challenged by so many people, and I don't frankly have time for total political correctness." Trump's stand against political correctness helps explain why all of his sexist and racist and insulting and offensive comments did not destroy his candidacy, as would have happened to many other candidates. Trump turns his offensive statements into a heroic act of resistance against the forces of political correctness. Even when people dislike what he says, they support the idea of someone who is willing to offend the establishment in every way.

As former KKK leader David Duke wrote about Trump, "I think he deserves a close look by those who believe the era of political correctness needs to come to an end." The brilliance of Trump's anti-PC maneuver is that it allows him to excuse every bigoted comment he makes. Trump declares, "I refuse to be politically correct," and his supporters cheer his courage, even though it mostly means that he refuses to stop insulting women and minorities.

In an era of scripted candidates with carefully focus-grouped phrases, Trump seems refreshing and different. In a Republican Party dominated by corporate interests, Trump's populist rhetoric seems like something new. But this is a careful disguise, not a genuine belief. Like past masters of populism, Trump tells the public what they want to hear, but only in order to get himself power. He has no core beliefs beyond his absolute convictions about his own greatness. For a man willing to make any deal to increase his power and wealth, it's almost impossible to know what he actually will do as president. The genius of Trump has been to turn that ideological uncertainty in an advantage.

Trump's fans use his narcissism as an excuse to dismiss any flaw. If you dislike one of Trump's ideas, it's easy to say that Trump doesn't really intend to enact it because it's all for show. If you have a policy you want enacted, it's possible to imagine Trump as the only one who can get it accomplished, thanks to his grand promises.

DID THE LEFT CREATE TRUMP?

Some conservatives blame politically correct leftists for creating an environment where Donald Trump might thrive. *Daily Beast* commentator Tom Nichols argued, "To understand Trump's seemingly effortless seizure of the public spotlight, forget about programs, and instead zero in on the one complaint that seems to unite all of the disparate angry factions gravitating to him: political correctness. This, more than anything, is how the left created Trump." For conservatives desperate to find someone else to blame for causing Republicans to nominate an unprincipled idiot, politically correct leftists are a convenient target.

But actually, it's the American right that created the fear of political correctness. The right nurtured this paranoia and stoked it with an ongoing attack on any leftist opinions for being "politically correct." Trump is their Frankenstein.

The right spread the myth of political correctness, the idea that leftists control all colleges and other social institutions, and that the only victims of political repression are conservatives. This ignores the fact that the most repressive colleges in America are conservative Christian ones, and that those colleges are the ones where devout Christians are the most likely to be punished for their (too liberal) beliefs. The right ignores the fact that leftists are still more regularly banned, fired, punished, and silenced on college campuses than conservatives are. And, of course, in the real world the people in charge look (and act) a lot more like Donald Trump. Everywhere white men think that they're an oppressed minority, there you can find the core of Trump supporters and the fundamental delusion about inequality in America.

Trump realized that he was better than the establishment at using the rhetoric of white male fear, and he could simply attack immigrants and free trade to build a link between both the racial resentments of these voters and their beliefs about economic self-interest. But Trump's appeal goes far beyond policy. It is precisely his politically incorrect approach that gets him so many enthusiastic fans among conservative white men.

Political correctness does unite Trump's supporters: rich white men who feel under attack in a more diverse era and poor white men who feel like someone stole their economic opportunities. The core of Trump's appeal is nostalgia. "Make America Great Again!" is a slogan stolen from Ronald Reagan and used to evoke a simpler era in the distant past, when white guys were in charge, America was respected and feared, and nobody worried about diversity. Even when Trump disparages America, he evokes the nostalgic dreams of a country before political correctness took over. Trump is always careful never to specify a date when America used to be great, perhaps because many of his fans might point to the late 1990s when a President Clinton was in office.

TRUMP AND
THE WAR HEROES

Many political analysts believed that Trump's attack on John McCain in 2015 would mark the beginning of his downfall. At the Family Leadership Summit, Trump declared, "He's not a war hero. He was a war hero because he was captured. I like people who weren't captured." (Immediately after the event, Trump denied ever saying that McCain wasn't a war hero: "If somebody's a prisoner, I consider them a war hero.")

But to everyone's amazement, Trump survived this unscathed, even though it should have alienated Trump's pro-military fans to see him attacking a soldier purely for being imprisoned (and tortured) for more than five years. Worse yet, while McCain was held prisoner, Trump was avoiding military service with student deferments and a medical deferment because of a bone spur in his foot (when asked which foot, Trump told a reporter to look it up in the records because he couldn't remember). It is impossible to imagine any other politician making a gaffe this terrible and suffering no political consequences.

Political incorrectness explains why Trump survived and even prospered despite his crude attack on a war hero. Even though virtually all of Trump's supporters disliked his attack on McCain, they liked his confrontational attitude. Trump also attacked Gold Star father Khizr Khan, whose son was killed in Iraq. Khan criticized Trump during the Democratic National Convention, asking what sacrifices Trump had made, and holding up his copy of the Constitution to offer to lend it to Trump. Trump sneered, "Who wrote that? Did Hillary's script writers write it?" (Khan's speech was one of the very few at either political convention that wasn't scripted.) Then Trump attacked Khan's wife, Ghazala: "She probably, maybe she wasn't allowed to have anything to say."

If Trump is willing to attack the most sacred of sacred cows, a tortured and wounded veteran or the parents of a dead soldier, then that means he may go after any politician or powerful member of the establishment. Trump may not be likable, but his supporters want a vicious attack dog, even if they don't agree with all of his targets.

FIGHTING THE PC POLICE

Roger L. Simon, former CEO of PJ Media, said about Trump's appeal, "He's unafraid. He's upbeat. He's funny. He despises political correctness." In reality, there's little sign of a sense of humor in Trump. Trump is just a bad insult comic, a guy who thinks being mean is good for a laugh. Calling Elizabeth Warren "Pocahontas" is about as close to witty repartee as Trump gets. Most people laugh at Trump rather than laugh with him. Much of the time, Trump is just a petty, vicious, angry man. But because Trump is willing to be outrageous, even if he's not hilarious, he's seen as a hero.

Going after political correctness allows Trump to wear the mantle of victimhood, and to offer that same status to his supporters. This transforms Trump's offensive comments into a principled act of resistance against the establishment. It also reinforces Trump's status as a rebel, a man courageous enough to offend those in power. Some voters then view the election as a referendum on the protests against him. If you oppose these disruptive protests, then you have to vote for Trump.

POLITICAL CORRECTNESS
AND DISCRIMINATION

The attacks on "political correctness" are especially appealing to the straight white men who believe, despite all the evidence to the contrary, that they are an oppressed minority. The tale of the oppressed white male fueled the rise of Donald Trump.

Trump claims that women have it easier than men in today's culture because men are "petrified to speak to women anymore." Of course, there's no actual evidence that men are silenced by political correctness, and many women can report the fact that men do in fact speak to them, including the kind of offensive sexist comments that Trump seems to prefer. But by promoting the idea that men are oppressed, Trump is playing to his core supporters.

When asked if Trump would be willing to choose a female or minority candidate, top advisor Paul Manafort rejected the idea, saying "that would be viewed as pandering." In reality, Trump is pandering to his constituency of white men who feel oppressed. Choosing a woman or a minority would ruin Trump's white male brand. When Trump's top adviser, the man supposedly devoted to making him act more presidential, announces that women and minorities will never be considered on a ticket with Trump, it shows the bigoted foundations of his campaign.

Trump could not win the Republican nomination at any other political moment. He needed the simultaneous hatred of government, the disgust with deadlock in Washington DC, and the pool of resentment at how the Bush Recession devastated the American economy. Obama became an easy scapegoat for the fears and failings of many poorer white people, and Trump became their savior. As David Brooks noted, "Trump represents the spread of something brutal. He takes economic anxiety and turns it into sexual hostility. He effectively tells men: You may be struggling, but at least you're better than women, Mexicans and Muslims."

THE SYMBOLS OF POLITICAL CORRECTNESS

Trump is fond of seizing upon symbolic issues. What might seem to pundits like a distraction or Trump's misguided focus on trivial issues is really Trump's way of reinforcing his devotion to fighting progressive culture. Trump condemned plans to put Harriet Tubman on the $20 bill as "pure political correctness." He declared: "Andrew Jackson had a great history." Great might not exactly be the word to describe a president who supported slavery and established the Indian Removal Act and the Trail of Tears that killed thousands of Native Americans.

Trump argued, "I would love to see another denomination" for Tubman. Trump suggested, "maybe we do the $2 bill," seemingly unaware that Thomas Jefferson, a far greater figure than

Jackson, is on the $2 bill. Trump apparently wanted to put the black woman on a bill that nobody uses, but since he never uses a $2 bill, he didn't realize that one of the most admired founding fathers was already occupying it. However, Trump seems to have an unusual desire to take things from Jefferson, since he recently said, "I want a statue in Washington, D.C. Maybe share it with Jefferson or somebody."

Denouncing "political correctness" is an effective way of marketing bigotry. Whenever Trump wants to say something offensive based on gender or race, he simply declares that he would like to say this offensive thing, but it's not politically correct. He depicts himself as a victim of some invisible force while he's victimizing someone else with a vile statement.

Trump wrote, "I never worry about being politically correct." In reality, Trump worries about it a lot. He intentionally takes controversial stands in order to strengthen his politically incorrect credentials.

THE HIDDEN SATIRE OF DONALD TRUMP

Being politically incorrect becomes a ploy to excuse bigotry or ignorance. Rush Limbaugh claimed that Trump's tone-deaf racial comments were actually incisive satire: "People just don't get it. Trump said 'I love Hispanics' while eating from a taco bowl, right?

... Jeb Bush said that's like somebody eating a watermelon saying I love black people or eating fried chicken saying I love black people. You don't get it. Trump's putting everybody on. Did you did you see the excrement-eating grin on his face? He's got the fork poised over the taco bowl. 'I love Hispanics!' And everybody, 'Oh, my God,' is having the vapors. 'He's being racist! He's being... Oh, no. No.' He's laughing at everybody, and the people that are supposed to be offended by this are laughing, too. That's what everybody is missing."

Trump makes an embarrassing racial gaffe by declaring that he shows his love for Hispanics by eating a taco bowl on Cinco de Mayo, and his political incorrectness excuses it. Limbaugh's implausible interpretation is that Trump is really a genius of subtle irony, who engages in racial insensitivity in order to humiliate liberals by showing how oversensitive they are. Trump does something incredibly stupid, and Limbaugh tells us that he's really being a brilliant satirist using his fake racism to humiliate the liberals who attack him. It's all a joke, Limbaugh claims. When Trump called for Russia to hack Hillary Clinton's emails, he reacted to the backlash by claiming that it was "sarcasm." Political incorrectness provides a veil to conceal bigotry. Every offensive comment can be excused as irony, to get a reaction from PC liberals.

Conservatives were angry at Limbaugh for embracing Trump. Travis Hale wrote, "Limbaugh is a mind-numbing, frustrating hypocrite. His tacit endorsement of Trump, now occurring daily during his show, is almost impossible to understand." Matt Lewis accused Limbaugh of "abdicating" his "responsibility" and lacking the "intellectual honesty and moral courage" of local Wisconsin talk show hosts who attacked Trump.

Limbaugh acknowledged that Ted Cruz was the true conservative voice in the Republican primary. But Limbaugh also expressed support for Trump at times and refused to denounce him. Limbaugh loves Trump because they are so similar: arrogant, provocative, politically incorrect. Limbaugh, in his heart, is more of an anti-liberal than a pro-conservative. He is motivated more by what he hates than what he believes in. Trump is the same way. And just as Limbaugh sometimes mocks his own audience, he saw something similar in Trump: "Trump knows he's putting everybody on and the trick is that he knows his audience knows."

Limbaugh also is a master of the politically incorrect technique for getting to have your racist cake and eat it, too. Trump can communicate a racist message to his most bigoted supporters. Simultaneously, he gets to say that it's not really racist but a commentary on the leftists who see racism everywhere. Political incorrectness is a way for bigots to enjoy their bigotry, deny that it's bigoted, and depict themselves as the victims of dishonest leftists.

PROTESTING TRUMP

Protesting Donald Trump by interrupting his speeches, blockading streets, or demanding censorship of his supporters is almost certain to backfire. The reason is that it confirms Trump's claims that he is a victim of bias and unfair treatment, that the politically correct are repressing him.

At Skidmore College, the campus Bias Response Group concluded that when "Make America Great Again" was written on the whiteboards of two non-white faculty members, these were "racialized, targeted attacks intended to intimidate." At Emory University, some students complained about being traumatized by seeing "Trump 2016" chalked on sidewalks around campus. They staged a protest to Emory's president, chanting, "Come speak to us, we are in pain!" These students argued that because Trump is a bigot, support of bigotry should not be allowed on campus. Trump is a bigot, but the idea of banishing support for one political party's candidate from a college campus is a frightening attack on free speech. Although no one was punished for writing pro-Trump slogans, these misguided attacks only reinforce the delusions of persecution that motivate some of his supporters.

A small number of advocates of repression on the left have made things worse, and provided evidence to support this myth by encouraging censorship and occasionally succeeding in their aims. Political incorrectness also helps explain why Trump's best chance to win the presidency comes from the people protesting against Trump. If the protests against Trump turn violent and suppress free speech, it could create a backlash that helps gain votes for Trump. The riots at the 1968 Democratic National Convention helped Richard Nixon win the presidency on a platform of enforcing law and order, and any repetition of that disorder would probably benefit Trump. The fact that the worst attacks in 1968 came from a police riot only helps prove why leftist campaigns based in any violence are doomed to failure.

If the 2016 election is a referendum on Trump, it will be difficult for him to win with all the baggage of bad ideas that he carries. But if a vote for Trump becomes transformed into a vote against the PC police who try to silence him and his supporters, then Trump gains dramatically. Trump's worst enemies are the best allies he can hope for.

As leftist writer David Moberg noted about a protest in Chicago, "Many Trump opponents, from petition signers trying to deny Trump use of the venue to protesters at the rally, wanted to stop Trump from speaking. That's always tempting when someone is saying things as stupid and insulting as Trump does on a regular basis. But it's the wrong response. . . . The left should not embrace an approach that could be seen as mimicking in any way Trump's hostility to free speech and incitement to violence or suppression of opponents."

Marilyn Katz responded, "Moberg is wrong. It isn't that the demonstrators meant to stop Trump from speaking . . . " But quite clearly some demonstrators did and do want to stop Trump from speaking (and succeeded in their misguided aims, and celebrated their success).

The people who want to censor Trump, ban him from speaking, or blockade a road to stop people from hearing him aren't expressing opposition to Trump. They're feeding the feelings of oppression felt by Trump supporters. They're giving credence to a delusion, the delusion that the PC police control everything, that Trump is the man who can defeat them.

A protest movement can bring attention to an issue being ignored by the media and the public. But that's not a problem with Donald Trump. A disruptive protest can feel more satisfying to its participants than the hard work of persuading Trump's supporters that he is a lying, bigoted, and dangerous idiot.

THE DARK SIDE OF POLITICAL INCORRECTNESS

Hatred is the foundation of the backlash against political correctness. For anyone angry at their unemployment status who sees illegal immigrants taking low-wage jobs, Trump is the answer. For anyone upset that black people are protesting against the police, Trump is the answer. For anyone pissed off that their incompetent boss is a woman or a minority, Trump is the answer. For anyone longing for the good old days when white men ran everything and said whatever they wanted to, Trump is the answer.

There is a darker side to the war on political correctness. In April 2016, Trump posed for a photo with William S. Lind while holding a copy of Lind's book, *The Next Conservatism*. That book served as an inspiration for one of the worst terrorist attacks in recent times, the 2011 Norway massacre of 77 people, mostly teenagers, by neo-Nazi Anders Behring Breivik, whose political manifesto plagiarized large parts of Lind's book. Lind denounced "political correctness" as a product of "cultural Marxism," and a Communist (and Jewish, as Lind explained at a Holocaust denier conference) attack on Christian America. The conspiracy theory about "cultural Marxism" was the fundamental doctrine behind Breivik's attack. The embrace of Trump by so many white supremacists reflects not only their agreement with his racist policies, but also an appreciation for Trump's willingness to speak out in defense of racist ideas and against the politically correct people who speak out against racism.

Most of Trump's supporters know in their hearts that he is a narcissistic, bigoted, even idiotic fool, but they see a vote for Trump as an act of rebellion. If you think the existing political system is worthless and corrupt, you'll vote for anyone promising to blow it all up. Trump's record at construction is mixed at best, with a long list of bad investments and misguided projects. However, he's always been great at demolition.

The Trump candidacy is like a student government election with a joke party candidate. The more that the administration and teachers (in this case, the pundits and the press) get outraged and tell students not to vote for the joke candidate, the more that students want to rebel against authority and vote for the joke. The difference, however, is that most people understand that student governments are powerless, but the presidency of the United States is a deeply powerful office, no matter how bad the political paralysis in Washington DC is.

The Oval Office is not a place for symbolic expressions of outrage, especially when they're based on a delusion of white male victimization.

THE PSEUDO-POPULISM OF TRUMP

Being politically incorrect helps a billionaire establish himself as anti-establishment and anti-elitist. Sarah Palin, perhaps the model of the pseudo-populist "regular folks" politician, said about Trump: "it's amazing, he is not elitist at all." According to Palin, "He's spent his life with the workin' man." Being the boss and ordering around your chauffeur and butler and other employees is not what most people imagine to be spending your life with the "workin' man." It's like praising Thomas Jefferson for spending part of his life with black people.

Trump himself has said, "I don't get along well with the rich," although his entire life and career seems to prove the opposite of that. Because most of the poor and working class people he encounters are his employees who have to be nice to him to keep their jobs, Trump imagines himself to be well-liked by the working people. By contrast, most of the rich people he knows are customers or celebrities accustomed to fawning treatment, and because Trump is mostly obsessed with talking about himself, they don't always enjoy his company.

Even Mitt Romney, the classic example of the one percent, could claim to invest in businesses like Domino's Pizza, Sealy, Staples, and Sports Authority, places where the workin' man has shopped. By contrast, workin' men don't buy Trump condos, stay in Trump hotels, or golf at Trump resorts. Workin' men never bought any Trump Steaks from the Sharper Image catalog.

Trump is not only the candidate of the 1 percent, he is so rich that he looks down on the 1 percent for being too poor to merit his attention. His skyscrapers and golf course resorts are aimed at the top 0.01 percent.

The magic of Trump is that he gives the illusion of standing up for the little guy. You're a victim, Trump is saying. You're a victim of the Mexicans, and the Muslims, and the Chinese, and Wall Street, and the Democrats. You're a victim, he tells them, and I will protect you.

In reality, many of Trump's most devoted fans are the victims of people like Trump: corporate leaders who pursued profit over people, who used the cheapest labor even when it was illegal, who outsourced production to low-rate foreign factories whenever possible in pursuit of the best deal. A hypocrite who yells loudly enough can convince many people of his devotion to their cause. When a group of people feel disempowered, neglected, and under attack, they can conclude that an outspoken hypocrite is still the best outlet for their outrage. Trump isn't the solution to their problems; he's the cause of many of those problems, and often offers the worst possible plans rather than actual solutions.

As a pseudo-populist, Trump is taking advantage of dissatisfaction with an unfair economic system and a corrupt political system that benefits the rich and powerful. But instead of offering actual solutions to these problems, Trump prefers the politics of distraction, using political incorrectness as a tool for avoiding substantive issues.

Charles Kesler argues, "being anti-P.C. has, from the start, been the central point of his campaign. It proved a brilliant decision." According to Kesler, "Trump alone was willing, eager even, to embody political incorrectness, to own it, not merely to patronize it." The more offensive Trump was, the more he proved the depth of his willingness to fight against progressive values. David French, one of the conservative leaders of the Never Trump movement, observed: "I can't count the number of people who've told me they're for Trump because they're 'sick and tired of political correctness.' But fighting back with vicious, aggressive stupidity won't make America great again."

Trump used political correctness as a tool for dismissing any kind of moral opposition to his proposals. "We're fighting a very politically correct war," Trump claimed, because we do not torture terrorists and murder their families. Trump even praised some of the worst torturers: "Saddam Hussein killed terrorists. He didn't do it politically correct." For Trump, invoking political correctness allows him to smear the other side as weak and wrong without bothering to make an argument. Trump never explains why murdering innocent people is morally correct; he can simply dismiss the opposition as "politically correct."

Donald Trump is not a complex figure. Plumb the depths of Trump's narcissism, and there is nothing but superficiality underneath. What's more interesting than Trump himself is the reaction of the American people to him. Why are so many people drawn to Trump? Trump is a forbidden fruit. The more people are told it's wrong to vote for him, the more enticing the idea becomes. The more he is disparaged by the media and the establishment, the more attractive he seems to many of his followers. That's the lure of political incorrectness. Trump becomes a symbol of rebellion. If you dislike the status quo, then Trump is the perfect vehicle for your anger.

Comedian Bill Maher warned that Donald Trump's popularity was a "result of a backlash to political correctness." Maher argued that "none of that justifies embracing a dangerous buffoon simply because his lack of political correctness is cathartic." Trump is using political incorrectness as a tool for his own political ambitions, manipulating an alienated segment of the electorate and appealing to their most bigoted emotions.

CONCLUSION
THE TRUMP GAMBLE

On June 16, 2015, Donald Trump rode down the escalator at Trump Tower, following his wife, giving a thumbs-up and wiggling his short fingers at the crowd of actors paid $50 each to wear Trump T-shirts and wave placards.

One thing Trump learned from his business career is how to be unclear and confusing, a factor that helps him as a politician. If someone signing a business contract doesn't understand what they're signing, and the other side does, that's to the advantage of the one in the know. Donald Trump makes his business arrangements as complex and inscrutable as possible.

If Trump clearly stated what he believes and stood firmly behind his words, he would alienate many potential supporters. But Trump has also learned that talking can benefit him, as long as he rarely says anything of importance. Trump's stream-of-babble approach is highly effective because listeners want to imagine that Trump supports whatever they do. If he keeps quiet, or provides a clear answer, his potential fans would be disappointed. But verbose answers, using many words to say almost nothing, allow listeners to project their favorite answers upon Trump's simplistic template. Trump's worst political missteps have occurred when interviewers interrupt him, ask him simple yes-or-no questions, and repeatedly follow up when Trump inevitably fails to answer the question.

Trump promises jobs, telling his rallies, "You're going to have your jobs back," as if the presidency were an episode of *The Apprentice*, and the entire electorate were apprentices waiting to be given a job by Trump. But the whole point of *The Apprentice* is that there is only one winner, and only one job, and that job is serving Donald Trump.

THE WORKING CLASS TRUMP

Trump uses his working-class accent and attitude to be uniquely appealing. He is crude, crass, and unsophisticated, a Rodney Dangerfield at the country club, someone who is rich enough to belong to the elite but different enough to be a working-class hero. The more contempt that wealthy, educated, establishment leaders direct at Trump, the more appealing he becomes as a rebel figure to the working class. Trump is a poor man's caricature of what a billionaire looks like: constantly talking about being "classy," supermodels by his side, gold and marble everywhere, chandeliers in the toilet. Trump is a living, walking, talking stereotype, a fictional character brought to life who could never be in a novel without provoking critics to complain how unbelievable he is.

Rush Limbaugh said of him: "He's the only possibility of wresting control of the country back from the upper class that has seized it and at the same time has stopped working for all Americans. That's what Trump represents here." There's nothing better than a multi-millionaire touting a billionaire as the man to fight against the upper class, as if working class America was saying to themselves, "What we really need is a billionaire who runs golf resorts, you know, someone who will really fight against the upper class."

Trump claimed, "Nobody's fighting for veterans like I'm fighting for veterans." Back in 1991, Trump was launching a personal war against disabled veterans who were street vendors: "While disabled veterans should be given every opportunity to earn a living, is it fair to do so to the detriment of the city as a whole or its tax paying citizens and businesses?" In 2004, during the middle of the war in Iraq, Trump wrote, "Whether they are veterans or not, they should not be allowed to sell on this most important and prestigious shopping street.... The image of New York City will suffer."

Trump is just another rich guy. His accent and his tough-guy persona reflect his connections growing up with the mob-related construction industry, not reality. He had a newspaper route growing up, but his daddy's chauffeur took him around in the limo when it was raining. Trump's pseudo-populism is about taking populist desires among the electorate and manipulating them to serve the interests of the rich—especially one particularly rich guy named Donald.

From his early childhood to his first job collecting rent for his father, to his casinos, to his reality TV show, to his presidential campaign, Trump has been one thing and one thing only, and he is the best at it: he is a rich asshole. He might be the greatest rich asshole in history. He became famous for being a wealthy blowhard, having sex with models, and firing people on TV. Trump's greatest business achievements have consisted of forcing others to pay for his mistakes.

Trump's ghostwriter Tony Schwartz noted: "Lying is second nature to him. More than anyone else I have ever met, Trump has the ability to convince himself that whatever he is saying at any given moment is true, or sort of true, or at least *ought* to be true." Schwartz said of Trump, "He lied strategically. He had a complete lack of conscience about it." Trump is half-snake, and half-snake-oil-salesman. He's a con man who has deluded himself into thinking the con is real.

No major candidate for president in modern times has a worse record of criminal behavior than Donald Trump. Trump's business engaged in illegal race discrimination and Trump lied about it in an affidavit. Trump made deals with the mob, engaging in illicit racketeering to get his buildings built. Trump has regularly announced how he bribed politicians, demanding political favors in exchange for donations. Trump thinks that attacking Hillary Clinton as "crooked" is the best way to stop people from realizing how crooked he is.

THE TRUMP DOCTRINE

The Trump doctrine is really like a Rorschach test: everyone looks at the inkblot that is Donald Trump and sees something different. You can see a global interventionist who goes anywhere and everywhere to defeat terrorists. You can see an isolationist who will keep us out of foreign wars no matter what. You can see a tough-minded negotiator who will enforce his will upon China and Russia. You can see a status quo realist who is happy to work with dictators and never shake things up. A foreign policy full of contradictions is not an accident; it is, instead, a foreign policy designed quite intentionally to appeal to the widest range of the electorate. Trump is everything to everybody, a loud advocate of many contradictory approaches that cannot work together.

"America First" isn't a foreign policy; it's a slogan, and an especially simple-minded one at that. The original "America First" slogan came from the isolationists in the late 1930s. Some of them, such as Charles Lindbergh, openly admired Nazi Germany. The American First Committee strongly opposed giving aid to the British, and helped Hitler move forward to occupy Europe. Trump's foreign policy plan is all about Trump. As Andrea Mitchell put it: "He is completely uneducated about any part of the world." Trump said about Russian leader Vladimir Putin: "A guy calls me a genius and they want me to renounce him? I'm not going to renounce him." Trump's foreign policy is fundamentally based on narcissism.

Actually, when Putin was asked why he called Trump "brilliant, outstanding, talented," Putin denied ever saying it: "Why do you always change the meaning of what I said...I only said that he was a bright person. Isn't he bright? He is. I didn't say anything else about him." The word "bright" in Russian can mean something closer to "colorful" or "flamboyant." It doesn't mean brilliant and it certainly doesn't mean a genius, as Trump misinterpreted it.

Trump bragged about Putin, "I got to know him very well because we were both on *60 Minutes*, we were stablemates, and we did very well that night." In 2014, Trump declared: "I was in Moscow recently and I spoke, indirectly and directly, with President Putin, who could not have been nicer."

Suddenly in 2016, Trump announced: "I never met Putin, I don't know who Putin is. He said one nice thing about me. He said I'm a genius." Trump often hears things Putin never said: "I was shocked to hear him mention the N-word. You know what the N-word is, right? He mentioned it. I was shocked." Although Trump blamed Obama for causing this "lack of respect," it turns out that Trump was the only one who ever heard Putin say the N-word about Obama. But Trump apparently hallucinated entire meetings with Putin, as well as inventing Putin's words.

Because Trump has taken contradictory positions on most policy issues, everyone agrees with Trump about many topics. Being Trump means being everything to everyone and absolutely nothing at all. Trump's promises are mathematically impossible: massive tax cuts for everyone, massive increases in spending on defense and infrastructure, no reductions in entitlements, and the elimination of the national debt. An analysis by the nonpartisan Committee for a Responsible Federal Budget found that Trump's economic plans would cause the national debt to almost double, growing from 75% of the entire economy today and going up to 127% of the economy.

In 2011, Trump indicated he would be willing to cut entitlements: "Many Republicans also miss the mark. They pretend we can just nibble around the edges by eliminating waste, fraud, and abuse and somehow magically make these programs solvent and pay off our massive $15 trillion debt." Conservative columnist Cal Thomas explained after a 2016 interview with Trump that "Trump's plan for reforming Social Security and Medicare, the main drivers of our debt, consists of eliminating 'waste, fraud and abuse' and growing the economy...." Trump 2011 mocked the plan Trump 2016 had for making entitlements solvent. So would Trump actually protect Social Security and Medicare as he now claims, despite his promise a few years ago for radical cuts? Which Trump do you believe?

Policies and ideologies are not important to Trump because they are impediments to his ambition. If he actually believed in anything, he could not have become the Republican presidential nominee. It was only Trump's deft ability to move with the political moment, to take any stand and then contradict it when public opinion shifted, that made him such a brilliant politician. Trump treats his beliefs like he treated his casinos: if any of them go bankrupt, he feels free to abandon them and move on to the next ideology.

Trump is the most Teflon-coated presidential candidate in history. No one has ever committed more gaffes, with fewer electoral consequences, than Trump. Most politicians present an image of total honesty and suffer in the public's mind every time they fall short of this model. But because Trump's image is all about exaggeration and shifting positions for tactical advantage, deceit helps his candidacy. No one actually believes that Trump is always telling the truth. So if a voter disagrees with Trump's stated position on abortion, taxes, foreign policy, and many other issues, it's easy to imagine that Trump doesn't actually believe in that disliked point of view, since he's probably stated a contradictory position. If you are sufficiently naive about Trump, it's easy to imagine a Donald Trump who agrees with you about almost everything. Normal politicians who are consistent and honest suffer the consequences from voters who disagree with them on a particular issue. Trump's moral flexibility encourages his supporters to imagine he agrees with them.

TRUMP'S POPULISM

Barack Obama helped created the success of not only Trump's candidacy, but also the even more astonishing success of Bernie Sanders' campaign. When the Great Recession hit America in 2008, it created a perfect populist moment: big banks ruining the economy and getting bailed out while the rest of America suffered.

The problem is that Barack Obama was not, and could not be, a populist. Neither was John McCain, his opponent in 2008, and certainly not Mitt Romney in 2012. Obama had risen to public prominence based on his soaring rhetoric of unity. He wasn't capable of shifting gears and suddenly becoming a populist, and racial resistance to his candidacy might have been overwhelming if he had adopted populist rhetoric.

Populist anger didn't disappear. It reared up in 2010 and put the Republicans in power around the country. But Mitt Romney was the wrong kind of candidate to take advantage of the anger bubbling beneath the surface of the American electorate.

That populist anger has taken hold of American politics in 2016, even though the moment of economic crisis that inspired it has passed. The American economy has seen growth in jobs for a record number of weeks, but Trump still must insist that unemployment is terrible and makes up fake numbers to support his claims and reinforce the angry feelings of his followers.

Jeb Bush argued that Obama's "divisive tactics" led to Trump because Obama "undermined Americans' faith in politics and government to accomplish anything constructive." Bush admitted that "a few in the Republican Party responded by trying to out-polarize the president." In reality, there was nothing divisive or unusual about Obama's rhetoric or tactics. In fact, Obama refused to use the populist rhetoric that Bernie Sanders showed was very popular. But the Republican Party, taken over by the Tea Party movement, adopted a stance of total resistance, refusing to pass legislation or approve appointments.

This fed the frustration with Washington, sent the approval ratings of Congress plummeting to record lows, and created the opportunity for an outsider who could claim to solve every problem and break every deadlock with his magical deal-making powers.

THE AUTHORITARIAN TRUMP

Research by Matthew MacWilliams found that a voter's gender, education, age, ideology, party identification, income, and race didn't have any predictive value in whether they were Trump supporters, but their authoritarian worldview did. Authoritarians value conformity and order, and when they feel threatened, they turn to aggressive leaders and policies.

Trump himself has an authoritarian personality. As Carl Bernstein noted, Trump is "a new kind of fascist in our culture" with an "authoritarian demagogic point of view." Trump admires authoritarian leaders such as Vladimir Putin. It's no surprise that Donald Trump retweeted a quote attributed to Mussolini, the Italian fascist leader: "It is better to live one day as a lion than 100 years as a sheep."

Trump already imagines himself to have the power of a brutal dictator: "I could stand in the middle of 5th Avenue and shoot somebody and I wouldn't lose voters." His mixture of populism, bigotry, conspiracy theories, authoritarianism, and far-right politics makes him a particularly frightening figure. Trump plays to the fantasies of his audience, but he also appeals to their fears and hatred.

THE TRUMP GAMBLE

With his casino background, Trump is an expert at attracting gamblers, people who are willing to throw the dice with the irrational hope it will make their lives better. Trump understands how to recruit gamblers—by evoking hope and concealing facts. A casino doesn't tell you that you're likely to lose; a casino tells you that anything can happen, and you might just win, and what the hell, you'll have some fun along the way. That's the appeal of Trump's campaign: take a chance on me, and I'll give you everything.

In fact, Trump literally promised "everything" to his followers. Trump promised workers in Michigan, "I'll get you a new job; don't worry about it." If the cost of supporting Trump is so small (a mere vote) and the potential economic benefits are so great (a new job, economic prosperity, and global dominance), why not go for Trump? Trump is the cheapest lottery ticket you'll ever buy. And even if the odds that he'll keep his word are very small, why not take a gamble on Trump?

This explains why Trump is so committed to denouncing America. He claims (despite all the evidence to the contrary) that the economy is a disaster, that the unemployment rate is really 42 percent, that everything is terrible, and that only he can make America great again. If you're trying to recruit a gambler, you need to make them feel like normal life is boring and miserable. Trump tells America that their lives are horrible, and even though it's factually not true for the overwhelming majority, they begin to wonder if he might be right. Everyone can imagine being richer and happier, and that's precisely the core appeal of gambling.

As Trump the real estate developer put it: "I play to people's fantasies . . . . The more unattainable the apartments seemed, the more people wanted them." Trump is applying the same principles to politics: Trump is presenting a fantasy of what people want from a president, and the more unattainable and unrealistic his promises are, the more people will want him even if they know they are being irrational.

Trump's own lavish lifestyle serves his message. Trump loves to have rallies at airport hangers; it's not just the convenience of flying in and out quickly. The true appeal of it to Trump is that it reminds his audience how incredibly wealthy he is: he has a giant plane with his name on it. Trump is telling supporters, I've got a plane. Do you? Vote for me, and who knows, maybe you will.

Might Trump's ostentatious display of extreme wealth turn off potential voters who are angry at financial inequality and the rigged system that favors the rich? The opposite is true: Trump is telling them the system is rigged and they're right to be angry at the rich, but Trump is the only one who can offer the salvation of getting rich yourself. Trump University was another form of shafting suckers gambling on Trump. Give Trump thousands of dollars to learn his secrets, and maybe, just maybe, you'll get really rich, too.

Trump also understands that the best way to bring people to a casino is with a distraction, and the best kind of distraction is a fight. A big boxing match attracts crowds who stick around to toss some coin at the casino. And so Trump is always provoking fights: with his opponents, with protesters, with the media, with Twitter critics, with anyone and everyone who irritates him.

Distraction is essential to any casino. You want bright lights and noisy machines, free drinks and sexy waitresses. You want fancy palaces with shimmering chandeliers. You want the customer paying attention to everything except the fact that it's all a giant, flashy scam. As the slogan of the Trump Taj Mahal says, "Excitement Returns." Distractions make people more willing to gamble. In an environment of calm analysis, rational thinking tends to prevail.

Trump explained his approach to *The Apprentice*: "I rant and rave like a lunatic and the crazier I am, the higher the ratings." This is also Trump's approach to his presidential campaign, because it is his way of life.

Casinos are a legal con. The gamblers always lose, collectively, and everyone knows that. But individuals can sometimes win. The key for any casino is to convince gamblers to imagine that they will be the exception to the odds. They don't even have to believe something so irrational is likely, they just have to hope.

Trump is gambling on the idea that he can convince the voters that the world they live in is a rigged game. They keep trying to play fair, and they get screwed. Trump is promising to play this rigged game, but says he will rig it on behalf of America. Nobody thinks Trump is an honest person; but the more he lies, the more his supporters can imagine that he's going to lie for us. He's going to be a lying son of a bitch, but he will be our lying son of a bitch. He's a con man working for us to take the rest of the world's money after they stole it from us.

The trick of Trump's con is that he implicitly admits to being a con man. Trump's book, *The Art of the Deal*, could easily have been titled *The Art of the Con*. The book is full of examples of how Trump misleads ("truthful hyperbole") and manipulates people to take advantage of them. Trump has bragged, "I've taken advantage of the banks probably more than any other human being on Earth." To Trump, conning people is a credential.

As a con artist, Trump believes in nothing but himself. Only a con artist could propose the largest tax *increase* on the wealthy in human history just a few years ago and now propose the largest tax *cut* on the wealthy in human history while simultaneously claiming that he's going to make the rich pay more. Trump will say anything to get elected.

Trump has only a few consistent positions that he has held for decades. Because Trump is a con artist, he will never believe in free trade. The concept of mutually beneficial agreements is alien to him; someone is always taking advantage of someone else in Trump's world. You're either the con artist or the victim.

The fact that Trump is a con artist does not mean he is plotting as president to steal a trillion dollars and run off to a remote island. Trump, after all, is a narcissist who dreams of being president and imagines himself the greatest leader in history. But Trump can never escape his con artist instincts. He is unable to change, and incapable of self-criticism. He will govern as a con artist, as someone who deceives and manipulates and seeks to control everything around him. As a con artist, Trump imagines that everyone is organizing a con as well, which leads to his conspiratorial thinking. Only the naïve fail to understand they're the victim of a con.

Casting a vote is as easy as buying a lottery ticket, and it's free, too. Why not take a chance that Trump can deliver what he says, even if you know he can't? The odds are against you, but hope matters more than probabilities. As the Powerball ad slogan says, "anything's possible."

Trump once said, "My life is like a game of poker." As a gambler, Trump knows how to take risks with other people's money. But he shows a dangerous tendency to follow instinct rather than reason. The only hope for Trump to emerge victorious is if he can convince the American people to be the same kind of gambler he has been.

Donald Trump is a pathological liar, a sexist pig, a hateful racist, a corrupt businessman, a pandering populist, a conspiracy nut, and a vicious bully. Trump's cynical narcissism explains why he wants to be president, but his political success reflects much deeper problems in America: the inequality of wealth that makes a man like Trump so powerful, the celebrity-obsessed media that gave Trump an uncritical platform for his ideas, and the failure of our political system to address America's flaws, which has allowed a bigoted demagogue to seize control of the Republican Party.

ACKNOWLEDGEMENTS

I want to thank Justin Humphries, John Oakes, Jen Overstreet and everyone at OR Books for their willingness to publish a book about a figure who suddenly dominated our political world, and for working so hard to produce this book under an unusually intense timeline. Thanks to the cover artist, Rachel Merrill, who did a fabulous job.

I also thank my partner, Lynn Haller, who has suffered through my obsession with all things Trump.

Finally, I must thank Donald J. Trump. Without Trump's crass stupidity, paranoia, bigotry, and pompous ignorance expressed without hesitation, this book would not be possible. If we're all lucky, he will be a blip in history, and this will be the last book he inspires anyone to write.

RESOURCES

In order to make this book easier to read, reduce the use of paper, and speed up production, all of the endnotes and sources are posted online with links at trumpunveiled.com and johnkwilson.com. The website will also include any updates, corrections, reviews, or responses from Donald Trump to the book. To contact the author, email trumpunveiled@gmail.com.

Trump's most noteworthy books are *Trump: The Art of the Deal* (1987) and *Trump: The Art of the Comeback* (1997), along with his most recent books, *Time to Get Tough: Making America #1 Again* (2011) and *Crippled America: How to Make America Great Again* (2015). It's important to remember that all of Donald Trump's books were actually written on commission by ghostwriters. They are sanitized fantasies of what Trump thinks he is.

But to understand who Trump is, you cannot believe him. Instead, you must look to his biographers, including *Trumped!: The Inside Story of the Real Donald Trump—His Cunning Rise and Spectacular Fall* (1991) by John R. O'Donnell (with James Rutherford); *Trump: The Deals and the Downfall* (1992) by Wayne

Barrett; *Lost Tycoon: The Many Lives of Donald J. Trump* (1993) by Harry Hurt III; *The Trumps: Three Generations That Built an Empire* (2000) by Gwenda Blair; *TrumpNation: The Art of Being The Donald* (2005) by Timothy O'Brien; *No Such Thing as Over-Exposure: Inside the Life and Celebrity of Donald Trump* (2005) by Robert Slater; *Never Enough: Donald Trump and the Pursuit of Success* (2015) by Michael D'Antonio; *The Making of Donald Trump* (2016) by David Cay Johnston; and *Trump Revealed: An American Journey of Ambition, Ego, Money, and Power* (2016) by Michael Kranish and Marc Fisher.

Those books focused on Trump's history as a businessman. This book has a different aim, to examine Trump's beliefs, policies, and character. I relied upon a wide range of reporters, commentators, and analysts of Trump (too numerous to thank) for pointing out important facts about Trump, and many of these writers can be found in the online notes for this book.

O/R **C**

Cypherpunks
Freedom and the Future of the
Internet
JULIAN ASSANGE with
JACOB APPELBAUM, ANDY
MÜLLER-MAGUHN, AND
JÉRÉMIE ZIMMERMANN

When Google Met Wikileaks
JULIAN ASSANGE

Kingdom of the Unjust
Behind the U.S.–Saudi Connection
MEDEA BENJAMIN

A Narco History
How the US and Mexico Jointly
Created the "Mexican Drug War"
CARMEN BOULLOSA AND
MIKE WALLACE

Beautiful Trouble
A Toolbox for Revolution
ASSEMBLED BY ANDREW BOYD
WITH DAVE OSWALD MITCHELL

Bowie
SIMON CRITCHLEY

Extinction
A Radical History
ASHLEY DAWSON

Black Ops Advertising
Native Ads, Content Marketing, and
the Covert World of the Digital Sell
MARA EINSTEIN

Beautiful Solutions
A Toolbox for Liberation
EDITED BY ELI FEGHALI,
RACHEL PLATTUS, AND
ELANDRIA WILLIAMS

Remembering Akbar
Inside the Iranian Revolution
BEHROOZ GHAMARI

Folding the Red into the Black
or Developing a Viable *Un*topia for
Human Survival in the 21st Century
WALTER MOSLEY

Inferno
(A Poet's Novel)
EILEEN MYLES